Programs

for

Lent

and

Easter

PROGRAMS FOR LENT AND EASTER

Copyright © 1979
Judson Press, Valley Forge, PA 19481

ISBN 0-8170-0861-6
Second Printing, 1981

The articles, programs, plays, pageants, worship services, background and sermon material, and other ideas found herein were originally published in the February, 1976; January, 1977; March, 1977; February, 1978; and March, 1979, issues of *Baptist Leader*. All the programs have been used successfully by churches across the country who have shared their experiences with us.

Programs for Lent and Easter

Compiled and edited by Vincie Alessi

Judson Press ® Valley Forge

An Easter Song

Before the sunrise,
A distant church bell
Woke me from my sleep.
Easter dawned.
I felt its splendor swell
The heavens with a joy
They could not keep.
Its victory song came
Ringing through earth's pain.
The Lord Christ lives!
The Lord Christ lives again!

Geneva M. Frost

Contents

The Promise of Spring

It's the promise of spring,
The expectation,
The hope and surprise,
The sudden elation,
From the very first burst of the daffodil,
The exhaltation
Of the purple hill,
The stirring of the earth,
God's celebration
Of new birth.

Elaine M. Ward

Worship at Easter

• **by Lynn and Virgil Nelson**

Possible Themes
- God's Power and the Resurrection
- One Must Lose Life to Find It
- Suffering Love: Our Call in Christ
- Forgiveness—A Fresh Start Each Moment

Preaching/Teaching
- Sermon by one or several, readings, music, slides, film.
- Reading of the "Warm Fuzzies." Claude Steiner, "A Fairytale" (35 Westminster, Kensington, CA 94708).
- "What Does Easter Mean to You?"—tape-recorded interviews with people in your church or on the street corner.
- Movement interpretation of songs, "A New Mind" and "Pass It On." Record: "Tell It Like It Is," R. Carmichael and Kurt Kaiser (Light Records, Lexicon Music, Inc., Waco, Texas).
- Film: *It's About This Carpenter* (12 min.) (Mass Media Ministries, 2116 N. Charles St., Baltimore, MD 21218).
- Slide show to Easter music.

Readings
Use as responsive, choral, or unison readings.
- Mark 15:42–16:6; Luke 24:13-35 (discovery of the resurrection)
- Galatians 2:20 (crucified with Christ)
- John 11:11-45 (Lazarus)
- Litanies from *Interrobang* by Norman Habel (Philadelphia: Fortress Press, 1969), $1.95.
- "You say the script is written?" Malcolm Boyd, *Free to Live, Free to Die* (New York: Holt, Rinehart & Winston, Inc., 1967).
- Before or during the service, ask people to write a paragraph for a good news paper.

Prayers
- Use silent, planned, or spontaneous prayer.
- Select readings from:
  —Norman C. Habel, *Interrobang* (Philadelphia: Fortress Press, 1969), $1.95.
  —Malcolm Boyd, *Are You Running with Me, Jesus?* (New York: Avon Books, 1967); *Free to Live, Free to Die* (New York: Holt, Rinehart & Winston, 1967); *Malcolm Boyd's Book of Days* (New York: Random House, Inc., 1968).
  —Michel Quoist, *Prayers* (New York: Sheed and Ward, Inc., 1963), $3.95.

Reprinted from *Respond, Volume 4*, edited by Barbara Middleton; Judson Press, 1975. Used with permission.

—Carl Burke, *God Is for Real, Man* (1966); *God Is Beautiful, Man* (1969); *Treat Me Cool, Lord* (1968) (New York: Association Press).

• Have group members write their own prayers beforehand, bring them, and read them as part of the service.

Fellowship

• Join in Communion, sharing in small groups, or action in a large group.

• Have a love feast. Have Scripture reading with the eating of bread, meat, grapes, and water (a simple meal such as the disciples might have had during Jesus' ministry). Sit in small groups (five to ten) around a tray of food.

• Consult your local synagogue for help in having a Passover Seder—the original setting for the Last Supper.

• Have foot washing in small groups, accompanied by Scripture (John 13:1-11).

• With flowers and arm movements, process or recess to "Joyful, Joyful, We Adore Thee."

Confession/Commitment

Confession and commitment can be private, public, or shared with a small group.

• Symbolically represent giving up the old self and becoming new:

—Have each person write on a piece of paper about one thing in his/her life that he/she wants to change and throw the paper into a fire. Have each one drink from a refreshing cup of water.

—Have each person record on tape one thing he/she wants forgiveness for and release from. Erase the tape and have the group listen to the erased tape.

• Music which might be used includes:

—"Standing in the Need of Prayer." Music: *Sing 'N' Celebrate,* compiled by Kurt Kaiser, *et al.* (Word Music, Inc., Waco, TX 76703).

—"Love Is Surrender." Music is found in the book mentioned above. It is also in the musical *Tell It Like It Is,* R. Carmichael and K. Kaiser, Light Records (Lexicon Music, Inc., Waco, Texas).

—"'Are Ye Able?' Said the Master."

—"Day by Day." Record: "Godspell" (Bell Records). Music: *Inspirational Songbook* (Hansen Publishing Co., Miami Beach, Florida).

• Have members of the group give testimonies concerning things their faith has given them the power

or strength to do.

Offering

• "Jesus in the Morning." Music: *Sing 'N' Celebrate,* compiled by Kurt Kaiser, *et al.* (Word Music, Inc., Waco, TX 76703).

• "Take My Hands." Record: "Sing, People of God, Sing," Sebastian Temple, St. Francis Productions (World Library of Sacred Music, Inc., Cincinnati, OH 45214).

Music for Celebration

Use solo, choir, congregational, instrumental, or recorded music.

• "Yesterday, Today, and Tomorrow." Music: *Sing 'N' Celebrate,* compiled by Kurt Kaiser, *et al.* (Word Music, Inc., Waco, TX 76703).

• "O Happy Day." Music: *Songs* (Youth Specialties, 861 Sixth Ave., Suite 411, San Diego, CA 92101), $1.25 each.

• "Sandals." Record: "Sounds of Celebration" (Zondervan).

• "Songs for the Easter People" (songbook) (Proclamation Productions, 7 Kingston Ave., Port Jervis, NY 12771), $1.00 each.

• "God So Loved the World." Music: *Come Together,* by Owens and Owens (Lexicon Music, Inc., Waco, Texas). Record: Light Records.

• "Lord of the Dance." Music: *Songs* (Youth Specialties, 861 Sixth Ave., Suite 411, San Diego, CA 92101), $1.25 each.

• "When I Think of the Cross." Record: "Cliff Barrows Presents Exciting Songs on the Way," Cliff Barrows (Light Records). Music: *Natural High* (Lexicon Music, Inc., Waco, Texas).

• "Magic Penny." Music: *Songs* (Youth Specialties, 861 Sixth Ave., Suite 411, San Diego, CA 92101), $1.25 each.

• "Weave Me the Sunshine." Music: *Songs* (Youth Specialties, 861 Sixth Ave., Suite 411, San Diego, CA 92101), $1.25 each.

• "Pass It On." Music: *Sing 'N' Celebrate,* compiled by Kurt Kaiser, *et al.* (Word Music, Inc., Waco, TX 76703).

• "Witness Song." Music: *Hymnal for Young Christians,* vol. 2 (F.E.L. Publications Ltd., 1925 Pontius Ave., Los Angeles, CA 90025), $5.00 each.

• "Amazing Grace."

• "Christ Arose."

Children, Death, and the Easter Event

● **by Richard Sammer**

When I was a child, I spoke like a child,
I thought like a child, I reasoned like a child. . . .
—*1 Corinthians 13:11*

For adult Christians, Easter is a day of unparalleled joy and celebration. Our hope as Christian people is rooted in the mystery of Jesus Christ—in his death and resurrection.

For young children not yet able to understand fully the story behind the Easter event, the death and

The Reverend Richard Sammer is a member of the staff of the Department of Ministry with Children of the Board of Educational Ministries, American Baptist Churches.

resurrection of Jesus Christ may appear contradictory or even meaningless.

How, then, can adults communicate the joy of Easter to those children within the Christian community? How can they share their beliefs with children and still leave them free to search for meaning and truth in their own lives? And how might children come to understand that Easter is more than a day for new clothes—more than a time for an Easter bunny, baskets, and colored eggs?

These important questions have been asked by countless parents, church school teachers, and Christian educators. What many do not realize, however, is that the search for answers to these questions must begin with them. Only if adults can come to terms with their own beliefs about Jesus can they adequately deal with the questions and emotional reactions of children.

Where Are We?

Let us reflect for a moment upon our own beliefs about Jesus. In her book *Helping a Child Understand Death,* Linda Jane Vogel lists several open-ended sentences, the completion of which may help us to focus our ideas and beliefs about this man Jesus. If we are honest with ourselves, the following can be an effective and helpful tool:

(1) Jesus . . .
(2) Jesus' death . . .
(3) Jesus' resurrection . . .
(4) The difference Jesus makes in my life . . .
(5) What I don't understand about Jesus . . .
(6) I am bothered by . . .
(7) I wish I believed . . .
(8) Most central to my faith is . . .

It is hoped that our beliefs about Jesus are a product of our struggle and growth in the Christian faith. But of equal importance to any knowledge we might have about this man is our motivation to share the faith that enlivens and enriches our lives. As adult Christians, our faith is transferred more through our living than any other fashion. Because Jesus' life and teachings continue to influence our lives, the joy we feel at Easter should be reflected in all that we say and do with children.

But What About Death?

When we are dealing with the events of Holy Week, the death of Jesus, quite naturally, is a frequent concern of young children. They may want to know, for example, why Jesus had to die. Or they may ask how a loving, caring God could allow his Son Jesus to be killed.

Questions of this nature may trouble adults as well as children, especially if adults have not come to terms with their own feelings and ideas about death. Certainly, as Christians, our beliefs about Jesus determine to a large extent what we believe about death. It may or may not be apparent, however, that our attitudes toward death will influence our answers to the children's questions about Jesus' death. Once again, the completion of open-ended sentences may help us to focus our ideas and feelings about this subject:

    (1) Death . . .
    (2) Dying . . .
    (3) Talking about death . . .
    (4) My death . . .
    (5) Death and life . . .
    (6) I am bothered by . . .
    (7) A funeral . . .
    (8) To me, eternal life . . .

Easter is a time not only to celebrate the resurrection of Jesus but also to remember that his death was *not* without reason. As we struggle to clarify our beliefs and express our feelings about death, we participate, as Jesus did, in the ultimate human endeavor. Given time, our faith may transform death from a problem to be solved into a mystery that points to eternal life. Belief in eternal life, of course, does not mean that death has become painless. Death is, and will remain, connected with real suffering and anguish—as it was for Jesus.

That is why it is especially important that we be prepared to answer the questions about Jesus' death as simply and honestly as we can, placing blame on neither God nor any ethnic group. Naturally, philosophical or theological interpretations will be largely meaningless to young children; but simple answers to direct questions will give reassurance and a sound basis upon which to build later questions and ideas.

Margaret C. McNeil suggests the following statement as sufficient to answer almost any question related to Jesus' death: "God did not choose that his Son should be killed. There were people who did not like Jesus. They were afraid of him. They were the ones who caused Jesus to be killed."

Children's questions related to Jesus' resurrection require a different response. Dr. Edgar N. Jackson believes it is wiser with young children to avoid the abstractions that tend to be meaningless to them. Any answer that we give to their questions must be geared to their level of comprehension. If we burden their consciousness with adult concepts, those concepts may be abandoned as children grow to maturity. If a child were to ask, "Why did God make Jesus alive again?" you might reply, "You will learn about that when your are older," or even, "What do you think?" Children often are able to supply satisfactory answers to their own questions when given the opportunity.

"I Don't Know "

Occasionally, children will ask questions which you cannot answer, When this happens, do not hesitate to admit that you don't know or that you don't understand everything about how God works. If it is appropriate, ask the children what they think. In this way, children may come to appreciate the mystery that is so much a part of life, death, and the Christian faith. They will benefit more from honest, open responses to their questions than from any number of half-truths or explanations that you yourself do not accept.

It is not uncommon, of course, for children to accept the events of Holy Week and Easter without questions. Faith comes naturally to them, and they can live with apparent contradictions far more comfortably than most youth and adults. The contrast between Jesus' death and resurrection—between the cross and the empty tomb—is significant, however, and can create problems for the young child—problems that may go unnoticed, How, then, might a concerned adult detect such problems?

To begin with, each child is different. This realization underscores the importance of having a meaningful relationship with individual children, a relationship that meets their particular needs for love, care, and being there.

Obviously, when dealing with the Easter event or any other occasion in children's lives which may provoke strong feelings or raise difficult problems, it is important to listen carefully to their questions and concerns. Often they are expressions of a child's confusion, anxiety, fears, anger, and even guilt. The use of pictures and music can be a way of helping children to become sensitive to people's feelings and of approaching any problems they might have, also.

Include the Children

Finally, and perhaps most importantly, children need to be included in any celebration of the Christian community. If your church has a traditional service or activity at Easter, adapt your schedule and resources to allow for the children's participation. If the children do not share in the worship experience, they might visit the sanctuary. This will give them an opportunity to realize something of the joy and pageantry of this special day.

Their inclusion in the preparation and celebration of Easter will communicate far more to young children than words or explanations ever will. They may speak, think, and reason as children; but they are a part of the Christian community. Like adult Christians, they rejoice in things which are alive; and, given time, they, too, will share in that Christian hope which is rooted in the mystery of Christ—in his death and resurrection.

Easter in the Kindergarten

● by Jean Lersch

Creating things to DO, without relying on reading, that also TEACH the Bible is the task for kindergarten teachers in church school. At Brethren House in St. Petersburg, Florida, the format described below has proven successful for the Sunday morning hour. The children come in, visit with the teachers, enjoy a presession activity, then gather in front of the chalkboard to hear an explanation of the day's learning centers.

"What're we gonna make today?" they ask.

And making something is indeed one of the parts of their session. The morning's routine is outlined on the board, and the teacher explains.

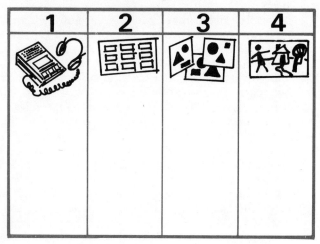

Jean Lersch is a member of Brethren House Ministries in St. Petersburg, Florida.

"Number 1 is a story for you to hear. You'll see two chairs at that table so that two of you can listen together. When you've finished, sign your name on the board here." And he points to the blank column under the drawing of a tape recorder.

"Number 2 shows a game you'll play. Bonnie will help you with the game. Then you can come back and write your name here.

"See the flannel boards at table 3? There you can make a picture of the Easter story. You can use those pieces on the table, and Sherry will want to see what you've made. Then when you've finished, what will you do?"

"Thign our name on the board," lisps Billy.

"Right! And at table 4 you can make something. I'll be there to help you. Now, remember, everyone will get a turn. What will you do if there are no more chairs at a table?" asks the teacher.

"Go to another onc," answers Ronnie.

"I'm glad you remembered. And I *know* you can take turns. You can start with any number. OK? You may begin."

And so the children choose their "work" at one of the four centers prepared for them. The success of the morning is due to the variety of ACTIVITIES attainable by four- and five-year-olds: there is *listening* accompanied by HANDLING: *handling* that relies on LOOKING; opportunity for *expression* using geometric shapes that spark imagination; and the *reinforcement* of the biblical event through the MAKING OF A HANDICRAFT with moving parts. And even before these four centers are to be used, the presession activity has announced the day's theme.

Presession Activity

Letters cut from Styrofoam meat trays lie on a table. They fit into the black outlines on a large green sheet of construction paper. And when they are all in place, the white message reads, "JESUS IS ALIVE." Of course, a teacher helps the first few children with the reading. But then she can stand aside as others arrive. Those who have put the letters in place can then proudly "read" the message to the newcomers.

Session Learning Centers

CENTER NUMBER 1—listening accompanied by HANDLING

An empty flannel board stands at the table along with a tape player, junction box, and two headsets. Lying on the table are six flannel figures gleaned from the sets of flannelgraph series in our resource room. Experience with tape players and headsets has taught the children how to operate this equipment. They know the color code of the adhesive tabs on the buttons: green for GO, red for STOP, and yellow for REWIND.

So the children sit at the table, put on the headsets, press the green button, and hear these instructions as they listen to the story:

Hello. You're going to be the teacher now and help me tell the story. Listen carefully and put the figures up as I tell you. If there are two of you, you can take turns. I know you won't have trouble taking turns because teachers know how to take turns.

Find the picture of the *big rock*. There's a tree in front of the rock and some flowers growing out of the cracks. Put that rock up on the board now. That is a tomb. It's like a cave. A cave in a rock has a hole in its side where you can put things. This is the place where they put the body of Jesus. You see, Jesus was dead. He died on the cross. His friends took him down from the cross and very gently wrapped his body in a sheet and put it in this cave.

They were sad to put him in there but glad they had a nice place to put the body. Now one of you pick up the *stone* that goes in that opening. You may have to work it around a little bit so that it fits. The soliders put this stone up in front of the opening so that nobody could get in. They didn't want anybody to steal the body. And they even sealed that tomb. That stone was so heavy that it took several soldiers to put it in place. So this stone was put in front of the opening to the tomb after Jesus' body was put in there.

Mary came to the tomb on Easter morning. She came to put some nice lotion on the body of Jesus. And she wondered about that tomb.

"Who will take that stone away from the door?" she wondered.

But something had happened. In the middle of the night there had been an earthquake, and the stone was now rolled away from the door. Take the stone off the board now. The stone was away from the door when Mary came to the tomb on Easter morning.

Find the *crying Mary*. She came to the tomb. Put her now in front of the tomb where she cried. Mary looked in the tomb and there was no body in there.

"What happened?" Mary wondered. "Did somebody come and steal the body of Jesus?" Mary was

very sad. She decided to go tell the disciples what had happened.

Take Mary off the board. When she told the disciples, "The body of Jesus is not in the tomb," they wondered what had happened, too.

Find the picture of *Peter and John* running. Put them beside the tomb. They are coming to see if what Mary said was true. "Wasn't the body of Jesus in the tomb?" they wondered. They went to see for themselves. So they ran to the tomb, bent down, and looked inside. Sure enough! She was telling the truth. There was no body in there. They wondered what had happened. Peter and John left to tell the other disciples. So take them off the board.

Put the *crying Mary* back in front of the tomb again because Mary came back to the tomb. She just couldn't stay away. She wondered what had happened to the body of her Lord. She was crying. Somebody came up behind her. Put the figure of *Jesus standing up* behind Mary. Mary didn't see who it was. She was crying and had her eyes closed. Jesus came up behind her.

"Why are you crying, woman?" he asked.

"Because somebody's taken away the body of my Lord," she answered.

Jesus then said, "Mary."

Mary recognized that voice. Could this be Jesus? She turned around and looked. Now take the *crying Mary* off the board and put up *the other Mary,* the one *on her knees.*

"Jesus," she said, "you're alive!"

"Yes, I'm alive," said Jesus. "I told you that I was going to die, but then I'd come back to life. I was in the tomb, but God sent an earthquake and raised me from the dead. Don't touch me, Mary. I'm going back to my Father. But you can go tell the other disciples that I'm not dead anymore. I have risen from the dead. I am alive!"

Mary was so happy. She did run off to tell the other disciples, "Jesus is alive! That's the reason I didn't see his body in the tomb. He came back to life. And remember, he said he would. Jesus is alive!"

That's what Easter is all about. We remember that Jesus is alive. Yes, he did die on the cross on Good Friday. But then he came back to life again. That's the Good News of Easter. Jesus is alive! Hallelujah!

In a minute I'll ask you to turn off the tape recorder by pressing the red button. Then you'll press the yellow button to get it ready for the next person. Take the figures off the board. I hope you were a good teacher. This is the end.

CENTER NUMBER 2—handling that relies on LOOKING

Scenes of Holy Week found in old curriculum materials were transformed into a matching game at this table. On a large piece of orange cardboard (21″ x 30″) are nine pictures glued in black outlined frames (5″ x 8″). The pictures, cut from old pupils' books, show (1) Palm Sunday, (2) The Last Supper, (3) The Garden of Gethsemane, (4) The Arrest, (5) The Trial, (6) The Crucifixion, (7) The Burial, (8) The Empty Tomb, and (9) Supper at Emmaus.

Identical pictures were glued onto 5″ x 8″ cards cut from the same color cardboard as the large background piece. The children's task is to lay the matching picture cards on top of the framed ones on the board. And a teacher is on hand to help when a child has difficulty.

"Look, David. What is Jesus holding in his hand?"

David scrutinizes the picture. He looks up. "Bread," he answers.

"Yes, now can you find the one on the board showing the bread Jesus is holding? Good." Calling attention to details helps the children with their matching task. And when all the pictures are in place, more reinforcement is possible.

"Let's look again at the pictures. *First,* Jesus rode the donkey into the city. See the palm branches the people waved. *Next,* he ate supper with the disciples. *Then* he prayed in the garden. . . ."

So pointing out the sequence of the pictures on the board reinforces the order of happenings during Holy Week. And being there to notice a child's work makes the effort worthwhile, especially when a child has difficulty.

CENTER NUMBER 3—opportunity for expression

Felt-covered masonite, measuring 9″ x 12″, bordered with colorful cloth tape provides an enticing background for creating an Easter scene. Small triangles, squares, circles, and rectangles cut from brightly colored felt lie ready on the table. Each child works to transform these shapes into an Easter scene like the sample standing against the wall.

"Look at my picture!" exclaims Brenda.

"I like that, Brenda. Tell me about it," asks the teacher.

"This is Mary. She's crying," explains Brenda.

"Why is she crying?"

"She doesn't know where Jesus is."

"Isn't his body in the tomb?" the teacher probes.

"No, he is not dead anymore, but Mary doesn't know that yet," explains Brenda.

"I guess that's what Easter's all about, isn't it?"

"Yep. I'm gonna go make the craft now." Brenda hurries to the empty place at the table marked with the number 4. She has shared her picture and is ready for more ACTION. So the teacher props Brenda's felt scene beside the other finished ones.

CENTER NUMBER 4—MAKING OF A HANDICRAFT with moving parts

At the craft table a teacher shows each child the sample. Printed at the top of a piece of oak tag (9″ x 12″) are the words "JESUS IS ALIVE." A figure of Jesus stands beside the outlined tomb. Rocks and other landscaping are drawn in the foreground. Over the tomb is a circle made from black construction paper, representing the rock. For each handicraft a slit, already cut in the oak tag, enables the child to slip the fastener through the center of his or her cut rock and the oak tag and bend the metal ends flat on the back. The paper fastener holding the rock in place allows the children to roll the stone away from the opening just as the earthquake did before dawn on Easter morning.

"First write these words, 'JESUS IS ALIVE,' Brenda. Then draw the other things you see. That's Jesus standing outside the tomb. Remember, he came back to life and came out of that tomb."

And while Brenda draws, the teacher checks with Eddie. "Let's see, Eddie, can you get the rock in place? Good. Now spread the ends of the fastener in the back. Now *you* can roll the stone away from the tomb. That looks fine."

Rolling the stone away from the tomb is fun. Inside the tomb the raised place where the body of Jesus lay is drawn. And some children very carefully add his grave clothes there. But Jesus is standing outside.

Bringing the Session to a Close

After the children finish all four centers, they gather again for their sharing and worship, including enacting the Easter morning scene at the tomb. The teacher calls them together by singing this song (to the tune of "Michael, Row the Boat Ashore"):

Come and see on Easter day, Alleluia!
Come and see where Jesus lay, Alleluia!
(repeat)
Jesus died but now he lives, Alleluia!
And new life to all he gives, Alleluia!
(repeat)

The children indeed have had, for the past forty-five minutes, things to DO, without relying on reading, that also TAUGHT the Bible. They enjoyed activities at four centers because the centers were designed to allow movement; each took only a short time; there was listening, seeing, and handling; teachers noticed, affirmed, and helped; and the children understood what to do. The moment of silence at the end of the period when the group "listened for thoughts God wants to give us" is rich with the sense of worship. A moment of silence to close is possible because planned activity had preceded it. □

Are you looking for a way to familiarize junior highs with the meaning and significance of Lent? Then the following is just what you need. It arrived at my office the other day. I was impressed with what one teacher had done, and I thought it might be something you would find helpful either as is or to spur your own creative thinking.

—the editor

Learning About LENT

• by Mary Ellen Ton

Dear Editor:

In the June, 1976, issue of BAPTIST LEADER, I came across the article "Can You Be 100 Percent Serious About a 60–40 Game?" I guess I can. Maybe I like to play the odds, and maybe I just feel strongly that I have something I want to communicate to kids—my faith.

Anyway—last Lenten season was for me one of those rare winners that keeps me hanging in there. I wanted to do something with the kids that would help all of us to catch some of the feelings of those persons involved in that original "Lent." So I tried to do this by focusing on the people involved and what their feelings might have been. My purpose was to help each of us to come to Easter with some feelings of identification with some people who lived and died a long time ago—most important, I wanted to help capture some feelings of what it must have meant for the man Jesus to *choose* to die.

Generally the class is a group of table drummers, foot stompers, and rubber-band-paper-wad tossers. Guess what? They really got caught up in those Sunday morning experiences. Not every one of them and not all of them at one time—no huge miracle, but a little one anyway—but enough to make me come away knowing why I am a church school teacher—and I must admit I wonder sometimes.

So I wanted to pass them on. They are not really original. Most of them are a collection of ideas and resources that seemed to fit together for me. Whether they have any value for anyone else or for another group of kids, who can tell?

Thanks for your share in helping to make us church school teachers feel that someone out there cares.

Shalom,

Mary Ellen Ton

Goals for Lent:

1. Junior highs should be able to recall the most important events leading up to Jesus' death.
2. Junior highs should be able to identify with the feelings of some of the persons involved in those events.
3. Junior highs should become acquainted with some of the customs of Lent.

Just to Get Us Started

Purpose: To begin thinking about Lent.

The author is active in the youth ministry of First Baptist Church, Evansville, Indiana.

To gather some information about an old Lenten custom.

Event: A pancake supper on Shrove Tuesday (None of the junior highs knew what Shrove Tuesday was.)

The junior highs were invited to my home for a pancake supper. We ate supper, played some table games (pool, Ping Pong, etc.), and some group games. The main game was a "Scavenger Hunt." The junior highs were given a worksheet with the following things to "find":

1. Find out what Shrovetide means.
2. Find out why we are having pancakes for supper.
3. Where does the word "Lent" come from? What does it mean?
4. When is Ash Wednesday? Why are ashes placed on one's forehead?
5. Find a place in the Bible where ashes (dust) were used for the same purpose.
6. Find out what "Mardi Gras" means.

Hidden around the room, visible yet difficult to spot, were clues written on slips of paper, as to where the answers could be found:

1. Encyclopedia
2. Encyclopedia
3. Dictionary and encyclopedia
4. Calendar and encyclopedia
5. Concordance
6. Dictionary

These resources were all available in different areas of the room. As the young people finished, we gathered together to share the responses. Then a story from *Creative Brooding** edited by Robert Raines, "Greater Love Has No Man . . . ," was read. The leader closed by saying, "I do not fully understand all about Lent and Easter. I do not really comprehend why it was necessary for a man like Jesus to die. But Lent comes again as a time to ponder the meaning of all of this and what it has to do with me. This is what we will be doing in class for the next several weeks leading up to Easter."

Session 1

Room preparation: Pussy willows, forsythia, bean seeds and bulbs; a large, bare branch, egg shells, watercolors; a large drawing of the outline of Jerusalem.

Presession activity: Paint symbols on eggs to hang on bare branch.

Approach: Divide class into three groups. Give each group a set of line-drawing cards,** along with these instructions:

   1. Identify what is occurring on each card.
   2. Arrange cards in chronological order.

[**Line-drawing cards can be made from old copies of *Good News for Modern Man*. Cut out and, using rubber cement, glue on 4" X 6" cards. These can be used over again in many different ways.]

When students have completed their work, list on newsprint or overhead projector those pictured events.

Development: Explain outline map of Jerusalem. Ask:

*Robert A. Raines, *Creative Brooding* (New York: Macmillan, Inc., 1977).

—Where was Jesus just before coming into Jerusalem for the last time?
—How can we find out? (Trace back from the triumphal entry.)
—Where was Bethany-Bethphage located in relation to Jerusalem? (Use a Bible atlas.)

Conclusion: Jesus' journey to the cross begins here—in Bethany. (Students can place on the outline map of Jerusalem the line drawing depicting an event that occurred there.)

[Teacher's notes: Students can trace the footsteps of Jesus throughout his last week on earth by using the outline drawing of Jerusalem and the line-drawing cards. Each week, as an event is studied, a new card is added. This is a good time to use the song "Lord of the Dance." It draws attention to the events of the last week of Jesus' earthly life.]

Session 2

Room preparation: Add as many pictures as you can find of the events in the last week of Jesus' life. Pictures coupled with thought-provoking questions can communicate much, i.e., a picture of Jesus as a small boy in the carpenter shop and a picture of Jesus on the cross, along with the question, "Whatever happened to the carpenter's boy?"; or a picture of the baby Jesus in the manger and a picture of the cross, along with the question, "Remember the baby that was born here?"

Presession activity: Continue to have eggs, paint, etc., available.

Approach: Your group may have consumed the larger portion of the previous session in identifying the line drawings and getting them in chronological order. If they did, you might begin the second session in the following manner (if they completed last week's session, then after a brief review, pick up at "Development"):

1. Where was Jesus just before entering Jerusalem? How can we find out? Divide into three or four groups, and assign each group one of these Gospel passages: Matthew 21:1; Mark 11:1; Luke 19:28-29; John 12:1.

2. Where was Bethany–Bethphage located? (Use a Bible atlas.)

3. Find a line drawing of something that happened there: getting the colt, anointing of Jesus, etc.

4. Place the pictures on the outline drawing of Jerusalem in the general location where each pictured event occurred.

Development: Listen to the recording of "Jesus Christ Superstar" beginning with Side 2 ("Hosanna" through "Poor Jerusalem"). It is a good idea to have the words available for the students to read as the record is played.

Form listening groups. Group 1 is to listen to the words of *Jesus,* Group 2 to the words of *Caiaphas,* Group 3 to the words of the *crowd,* and Group 4 should listen to the words of *Simon Zealotes.* Listen for the following:

● What are they communicating? What do you hear them saying?

- Do you think they are hearing each other?
- What makes you think they are or are not?
- Where do you see yourself? Are you Caiaphas, one of the crowd, Simon Zealotes, or do you identify with Jesus?

Conclusion: Add the line drawing of the triumphal entry. In quietness listen to the same section of "Jesus Christ Superstar."

Session 3

Presession activity: Decorate eggs. Learn "Lord of the Dance."

Room preparation: Secure a table large enough for thirteen seats. Have juice, bread, and cups.

Approach: Jesus was the host at a dinner. He invited twelve guests. Can you name them? (Look up "apostles" in the index of *Good News for Modern Man.*)

Using da Vinci's picture of *The Last Supper* in *Christ and the Fine Arts* by Cynthia Pearl Maus, identify the twelve apostles as they are shown around the table. Make name cards and place them on the table in your room in the order the disciples are in the picture.

Have available pictures of the twelve apostles, and let each student select one and take the place of that disciple at the table.

Development: When all are seated at the table and in complete silence, ask the students to use the response sheet. Share responses one at a time.

Conclude by sharing in the Lord's Supper:

The leader passes the bread and the juice to each person, saying: " (name), eat this (drink this) and remember Jesus."

Sing "Lord of the Dance" and end with prayer.

Response Sheet

1. If I had been present at the Lord's Supper when Jesus said, "One of you will betray me," I would have:
   a. felt guilty, because. . . .
   b. known that he wasn't talking about me, because. . . .
   c. pointed my finger at one of the others, because. . . .
   d. wondered if just maybe I might be the one he meant, because. . . .

2. Jesus invited his friends to eat this meal with him because:
   a. he wanted to accuse them of betrayal.
   b. he wanted to enjoy their company one last time.
   c. he wanted to tell them he thought he might be killed.
   d. it was a religious custom.

3. In the church today, we have the Lord's Supper because:
   a. Jesus said we should.
   b. we want to remember Jesus' death.
   c. it makes us feel close to God.
   d. it makes us feel close to each other.
   e. it reminds us of how much Jesus loved and needed his friends.
   f. I don't know.

4. When I participate in the Lord's Supper, I:
   a. feel uncomfortable.
   b. feel guilty and ashamed.
   c. sometimes feel very close to God.
   d. don't really feel anything.
   e. have a good, happy feeling.

Session 4

Students should be able to experience with their feelings what it meant for Jesus to "choose" death as they deal with some of their own feelings about their own death.

Room preparation: A life expectancy chart can be made in advance, showing the average life span for your age group; i.e., a male twelve years old can expect to live fifty-eight more years. (This type of information is easily obtained at any public library.)

Approach: Ask the students to draw their lifeline, indicating what they expect to be doing at various ages. A complete strategy for this activity can be found in *Values Clarification,** by Sidney B. Simon, Leland Howe, and Howard Kirschenbaum, page 304.

How did you feel and what did you think as you looked at your lifeline?

Development: Use response sheet that appears at the end of this session. After students have been given time to reflect on and fill out the response sheet, begin by sharing your answers and then go around the circle with each student sharing. (Using a response sheet seems to give the student more confidence in sharing his or her thoughts.)

Invite students to write their own obituary. They should write what they would like to have said about themselves if they died now. A complete strategy for this activity can be found in *Values Clarification,* page 311.

If enough time remains after the students have had ample time to share their obituaries with the group, they might like to try the same activity in writing Jesus' obituary.

Conclusion: Simply share with the students the difficulty we have in thinking about death, particularly our own. Sometimes it helps to gain perspective on life by contemplating death. We all have just so many years left, and we have a choice as to how we will spend those years.

Response Sheet

1. I think about my own death:
   a. sometimes.
   b. never.
   c. a lot.
2. When I think about dying, I. . . .
3. I am most helped in thinking about death when. . . .
4. I am helped the least in thinking about death by. . . .
5. I can raise questions about death with. . . .
6. The people I wish would talk to me about death are. . . .

*Sidney B. Simon, Leland Howe, and Howard Kirschenbaum, *Values Clarification* (New York: Hart Publishing Co., Inc., 1972).

the lent-easter story

A Way Your Church School Can Share It

• by Barbara Kraemer Clausen and William H. Bopf

Learning through doing—that's how many church schools tell the Christmas story through story and song. So why not the story of Lent and Easter, too? A church in Orlando, Florida, did just that. And it's here to share its Easter tableau, "The Week That Shook the World," with you.

The tableau, a series of slowly changing scenes, depicts the events from Palm Sunday through Easter, inside a worship setting. Over these pictures comes the Lent-Easter story—seen in the movements of the actors and heard through offstage narrators and "character readers," choral readings, and song.

All children in the church school participate—some as actors, some as readers, some as singers, some as scenery changers. Rehearsals are kept to a minimum by assigning specific responsibilities to each grade level and by narrators reading, not memorizing, the speeches.

The actors in the tableau do not speak, nor do they pretend to be speaking. Their presence and their deliberate, slow movements are all of the story they tell. The message in words comes through "character readers" and narrators who, though they are outside the spotlight, should be able to see the scene changes.

Darkness is an easy "curtain" to use for masking the change of scenes. With the lights out, characters take their places and "freeze." A spotlight then focuses on each scene as the narrator begins to read.

Since a darkened church is essential to format and impact, consider having the tableau Palm Sunday evening, perhaps late Maundy Thursday or Good Friday, or as your last Lenten service. You might even consider reviving the ancient custom of an Easter vigil on Saturday night—with the final scene and hymn of the tableau as your first celebration of Easter joy.

A few practical matters, then on to the script for the tableau:

• Kindergarten, primary, and middler classes (K-4) present their message in groups—songs, poetry, choral readings—while older children carry more individual responsibility in the tableau.

• How to divide up those individual parts? Look first at the talents of your teachers and students. If "Mrs. Allemani and her fifth graders" love art projects, perhaps they can design and paint the sets. Desire and

creativity can easily compensate for less developed artistic talent. If "Mr. Brothers's seventh graders" really take to drama and role playing, perhaps they're the "naturals" for the main acting parts.

• Since most of the characters in the tableau are male, you'll likely want to let girls take some male roles, too—but that's hardly a problem: The actors don't speak; plus most of the actors will look quite alike in their biblical costumes. And the use of groups of actors in scenes in depicting the mob in the garden of Gethsemane, the Sadducees, Caiaphas's council, and Pilate's courtiers make it possible to offer nearly every student a part in the tableau.

• Few acting directions are suggested. If possible, allow the actors to develop minimally their own actions to fit the narration.

• If possible, mount the spotlight in the balcony and use colored gelatin overlays to enhance the change in mood from scene to scene. Also, a balcony location for the spotlight will help keep this technical operation from distracting the congregation.

• Enlist the parents' help in making costumes and creating and collecting props. Old bed linens and ropes are a good start for costumes.

• Large packing boxes from appliances or discarded wardrobes from van lines can be used to make sets or backdrops. For Scene 11 you'll want a "rock" large enough to conceal Jesus at the beginning of the scene. Attach a sturdy but lightweight wooden support to the back of each flat of scenery.

For another scenery idea, draw the setting on large sheets of newsprint or wide tablecloth paper; fasten them to the dowel of a banner pole supported in a flag stand. You might design a number of huge paper "banners," one or more for each scene. Staple the sheets together on the dowel and flip over like calendar pages. If you have no banner pole handy, you can make one. Drill a hole slightly larger than the diameter of the dowel through a long broom handle, near the top of the handle. Push the dowel halfway through the broom handle, and set the pole in an empty flag stand.

• Since palms may not be as accessible to you as they are to the teachers in Orlando, see your florist about getting some of the brown fronds trimmed from potted palms. Or simply have each child make a courtly arm sweep to welcome Jesus' arrival, keeping the arm outstretched downward and head slightly lowered.

Reprinted from *Interaction*, April, 1976. © Concordia Publishing House, Saint Louis, MO 63118. Used by permission.

The Week That Shook the World

(Adapted from the Easter tableau at Trinity Church, Orlando, Florida, on Palm Sunday, 1974. Bible quotations are from Today's English Version of the New Testament. Copyright © American Bible Society, 1966.)

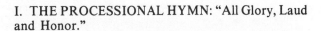

I. THE PROCESSIONAL HYMN: "All Glory, Laud and Honor."

(As all the children process, they form a line on each side of the center aisle. Jesus and his disciples come in last as children lay palms at his feet.)

II. THE LITANY OF REPENTANCE

Pastor: O Lord,
You who came to call sinners to repentance:
People: Call us still that we may answer.

Pastor: You who did meet the hardness of the thief:
People: Soften the hearts of all who are impenitent.

Pastor: You who did call Zacchaeus from the sycamore tree:
People: Arouse the careless and arrest the curious.

Pastor: You who did speak words of spirit and of life:
People: Enlighten the ignorant and teach the unlearned.

Pastor: Dispel all prejudice and correct all error:
People: Establish Your people in the truth of Your gospel.

Pastor: You who did pray for Your murderers:
People: Pity those who persecute Your servants.

Pastor: You who did call out many devils:
People: Set free by the power of Your grace the many who are the victims of pride and anger, of greed and selfishness.

Pastor: You who did satisfy the doubts of Thomas:
People: Deal gently with those who can scarcely believe.

Pastor: You who did uplift the sinking Peter:
People: Support all who are weak and unstable.

Pastor: You who did proclaim deliverance to the captives:
People: Pity all prisoners and loose the bonds of their sin.

Pastor: You who did raise the dead to life:
People: Quicken us all to life in Your righteousness.

Pastor: You who did come to save Your people from their sins:
People: Save, O Lord, those who put their trust in You.

Pastor: Save us, O Lord:

People: Deliver us, and purge away our sins, for Jesus' sake. Amen.

III. THE SCRIPTURE READING: Luke 18:31-34

IV. THE OFFERING

V. THE TABLEAU

THE HYMN OF INVITATION—"Go to Dark Gethsemane" or some other appropriate hymn. *(Lights in nave begin to dim.)*

Narrator 1: Today is Palm Sunday, the introduction to Holy Week, the most earthshaking week in the history of the world. The week begins and ends in triumph. The hosannas of Palm Sunday are recalled by the alleluias of Easter Sunday. The events that made such a difference in our lives occurred between these two Sundays. It is these events that we would like to present to you now.

SCENE 1—Monday: Jesus Cleanses the Temple (Spotlight slowly rising on "Jesus.")

Narrator 2: When they arrived in Jerusalem, Jesus went to the temple and began to drive out all those who bought and sold in the temple. He overturned the tables of the money changers and the stools of those who sold pigeons and would not let anyone carry anything through the temple courts. He then taught the people.

Jesus: It is written in the Scriptures that God said, "My house will be called a house of prayer for all peoples. But you have turned it into a hideout for thieves!"

(Spotlight out.)

Narrator 2: The chief priests and the teachers of the Law heard of this; so they began looking for some way to kill Jesus. They were afraid of him, because the whole crowd was amazed at his teaching.

SCENE 2—Tuesday: The Great Commandment

Narrator 1: Some Sadducees came to Jesus. They were the ones who said that people will not rise from death.

(Spot on.)

Sadducee: Teacher, Moses taught: "If a man who has no children dies, his brother must marry the widow so they can have children for the dead man." Now, there were seven brothers who used to live here. The oldest got married and died without having children; so he left his widow to his brother. The same thing happened to the second brother and to the third, and finally to all seven. Last of all, the woman died. Now, on the day when the dead are raised to life, whose wife will she be? All of them had married her!

Jesus: How wrong you are! It is because you don't know the Scriptures or God's power. For when the dead are raised to life, they will be like the angels in heaven, and men and women will not marry. Now, about the dead being raised: haven't you ever read what God has told you? For he said: "I am the God of Abraham, the God of Isaac, and the God of Jacob." This means that he is the God of the living, not of the dead.

Narrator 1: When the crowds heard this, they were amazed at his teaching. When the Pharisees heard that Jesus had silenced the Sadducees, they came together; and one of them, a teacher of the Law, tried to trap him with a question.

Pharisee: Teacher, which is the greatest commandment in the Law?

Jesus: You must love the Lord your God with all your heart, and with all your soul, and with all your mind. This is the greatest and the most important commandment. The second most important commandment is like it: You must love your neighbor as yourself. The whole Law of Moses and the teachings of the prophets depend on these two commandments.

(Spot out.)

SONG: "Jesus Loves Children" or some other song. *(Kindergarten and primary grades.)*

SCENE 3—Wednesday: Judas Agrees to Betray Jesus

Narrator 2: Then one of the twelve disciples—the one named Judas Iscariot—went to the chief priests.

(Spot on.)

Judas: What will you give me if I hand Jesus over to you?

Narrator 2: So they counted out thirty silver coins and gave them to him. From then on Judas was looking for a good chance to betray Jesus.

(Spot out while Judas is counting the money.)

HYMN: "Jesus, and Shall It Ever Be"
(Either by all the children or the congregation.)

SCENE 4—Thursday: The Disciples Prepare the Passover

Narrator 1: The day came during the Feast of Unleavened Bread when the lambs for the Passover meal had to be killed. Jesus sent Peter and John with these instructions.

(Spot on.)

Jesus: Go and get our Passover supper ready for us to eat.

Peter: Where do You want us to get it ready?

Jesus: Listen! As you go into the city, a man carrying a jar of water will meet you. Follow him into the house that he enters, and say to the owner of the house: "The Teacher says to you, 'Where is the room where My disciples and I will eat the Passover supper?'" He will show you a large furnished room upstairs, where you will get everything ready.

(Spot out.)

SCENE 5—Friday, 6:00-12:00 p.m.: The Upper Room

Narrator 2: According to the Jewish division of the

day, what is here presented as having happened on Friday occurred, according to our reckoning of time, from Thursday at 6:00 p.m. to Friday at 6:00 p.m.

It was now the day before the Feast of Passover. Jesus knew that his hour had come for him to leave this world and go to the Father. He had always loved those who were his own in the world, and he loved them to the very end. Jesus and his disciples were at supper.

(Spot on.)

The devil had already decided that Judas, the son of Simon Iscariot, would betray Jesus. Jesus knew that the Father had given him complete power. He knew that he had come from God and was going to God. So Jesus rose from the table, took off his outer garment, and tied a towel around his waist. Then he poured some water into a washbasin and began to wash the disciples' feet and dry them with the towel around his waist. Simon Peter reacted:

Peter: Are You going to wash my feet, Lord?

Jesus: You do not know now what I am doing, but you will know later.

Peter: You will never, at any time, wash my feet!

Jesus: If I do not wash your feet, you will no longer be My disciple.

Peter: Lord, do not wash only my feet, then! Wash my hands and head, too!

Jesus: Whoever has taken a bath is completely clean and does not have to wash himself, except for his feet. All of you are clean—all except one.

Narrator 2: Jesus already knew who was going to betray him; that is why he said: "All of you, except one, are clean."

(Jesus replaces his outer garment.)

Jesus: Do you understand what I have just done to you? You call Me Teacher and Lord, and it is right that you do so, because I am. I am your Lord and Teacher, and I have just washed your feet. You, then, should wash each other's feet. I have set an example for you so that you will do just what I have done for you. I tell you the truth: no slave is greater than his master; no messenger is greater than the one who sent him. Now you know this truth; how happy you will be if you put it into practice.

(Kindergarten and grade one make their contribution—poem, song, choral reading—standing in front of the church.)

(Chancel lighting off.)

SCENE 6—Friday, 12:00–3:00 a.m.: Gethsemane

Narrator 1: After celebrating the Passover in the upper room, Jesus went with his disciples to a place called Gethsemane.

(Spot on.)

Jesus: Sit here while I go over there and pray.

Narrator 1: He took with him Peter and Zebedee's two sons. Grief and anguish came over him.

Jesus: The sorrow in My heart is so great that it almost crushes Me. Stay here and watch with Me.

(Goes farther on and prays.)

My Father, if it is possible, take this cup away from Me! But not what I want, but what You want.

(The disciples meanwhile have fallen asleep. Jesus returns to find them.)

How is it that you three were not able to watch with Me for one hour? Keep watch, and pray so you will not fall into temptation. The spirit is willing, but the flesh is weak.

(Jesus again goes away and prays.)

My Father, if this cup cannot be taken away unless I drink it, Your will be done.

(He returns to the three.)

Are you still sleeping and resting? Look! The hour has come for the Son of man to be handed over to the power of sinful men. Rise, let us go. Look, here is the man who is betraying Me!

(Judas arrives with the crowd.)

Judas: Peace be with you, Teacher.

(Kisses Jesus.)

Jesus: Be quick about it, friend!

(The crowd holds Jesus tight.)
(Spotlight out.)

HYMN: "Twas on That Dark, That Doleful Night"
(Nave lights on for congregational singing—then off.)

SCENE 7—Friday, 3:00–6:00 a.m.: Caiaphas

Narrator 2: Those who had arrested Jesus took him to the house of Caiaphas, the high priest, where the teachers of the Law and the elders had gathered together. The chief priests and the whole council tried to find some evidence against Jesus to put him to death; but they could not find any, even though many came up and told lies about him.

(Spot on.)

False witnesses: This man said, "I am able to tear down God's temple and three days later build it back up."

Caiaphas: Have You no answer to give to this accusation against You?

(Jesus remains silent.)

In the name of the living God, I now put You on oath: tell us if You are the Messiah, the Son of God.

Jesus: So you say. But I tell all of you: From this time on you will see the Son of man sitting on the right side of the Almighty and coming on the clouds of heaven!

Caiaphas: Blasphemy! We don't need any more witnesses! Right here you have heard his wicked words! What do you think?

Council: He is guilty and must die.

(Spot out.)

SONG: "Jesus Walked This Lonesome Valley" or some other appropriate song.
(Upper grades.)

SCENE 8—Friday, 6:00-9:00 a.m.: Pilate

Narrator 1: They took Jesus from Caiaphas's house to the governor's palace. It was early in the morning.

(Spot on.)

Pilate: Are You the king of the Jews?

Jesus: Does this question come from you, or have others told you about Me?

Pilate: Do you think I am a Jew? It was Your own people and their chief priests who handed You over to me. What have You done?

Jesus: My kingdom does not belong to this world; if My kingdom belonged to this world, My followers would fight to keep Me from being handed over to the Jews. No, My kingdom does not belong here.

Narrator 1: The crowd became angry and shouted:

People *(offstage):* If you set him free, that means you are not the emperor's friend! Anyone who claims to be a king is the emperor's enemy. Kill him! Kill him! Nail him to the cross! The only king we have is the emperor!

Narrator 1: Then Pilate handed Jesus over to them to be nailed to the cross.

(Spot out.)

SONG: "Were You There?"
(Upper grades.)

SCENE 9—Friday, 9:00 a.m.-3:00 p.m.: Crucifixion

Narrator 2: It was nine o'clock in the morning when they nailed him to the cross. The notice of the accusation against him was written, "The King of the Jews."

(Spot on.)

At noon the whole country was covered with darkness,

which lasted for three hours. At three o'clock Jesus cried out:

Jesus: My God, My God, why did you abandon Me?

Narrator 2: And with a loud cry, Jesus died.

(Grades two and three make their contribution.)
(Spot stays on.)

SCENE 10—Friday, 3:00-6:00 p.m.: Burial

Narrator 1: Joseph, who was from the town of Arimathea, asked Pilate if he could take Jesus' body. Pilate told him he could have the body; so Joseph went and took it away.

(Spot out.)

Joseph and Nicodemus took Jesus' body and wrapped it in linen cloths with spices; for this is how the Jews prepare a body for burial. There was a garden in the place where Jesus had been put to death, and in it there was a new tomb where no one had ever been laid. Since it was the day before the Jewish sabbath, and because the tomb was close by, they laid Jesus there.

SCENE 11—Sunday: Resurrection

(Spot on.)

Narrator 2: Mary Magdalene stood crying outside the tomb. She turned around and saw Jesus standing there, but she did not know that it was Jesus.

Jesus: Woman, why are you crying? Who is it you are looking for?

Mary: If you took him away, sir, tell me where you have put him, and I will go and get him.

Jesus: Mary!

Mary: Master!

Jesus: Do not hold on to Me, because I have not yet gone back up to the Father. But go to My brothers and tell them for Me, "I go back up to him who is My Father and your Father, My God and your God."

(Lights in the nave are gradually turned on.)

Narrator 2: So Mary Magdalene told the disciples that she had seen the Lord and that he had told her this. As Mary went to spread the word of Christ's resurrection, let us go and tell others that Christ is indeed risen from the dead, lives, and reigns forever.

BENEDICTION
(Spoken by all the children.)

Now may God, who brought forth Jesus from the grave, be with us and bless us throughout all ages. Amen.

RECESSIONAL HYMN—"The Day of Resurrection" or "Christ the Lord is Risen Today."

Palm Sunday Fair

● by Monica A. Brown

While searching for a new way to teach our senior high class about Lent and the events of Holy Week, my co-teacher, David Given, and I hit upon the idea of a Lent Event which we and the senior highs chose to call Palm Sunday Fair.

We spent the Sunday class periods from Ash Wednesday to Palm Sunday preparing for the event. The young people prepared collages depicting the words "crucifixion" and "resurrection" today and displayed the collages along with cinquain poetry written by the senior highs about Lent to publicize the coming event to the congregation.

The senior highs then prepared games that would teach others about Lent and Holy Week. Grades three to eight were invited to join the senior highs on Palm Sunday during their regular church school hour to participate in the fair. Adults and younger children of the congregation joined the group during the fellowship hour after the class. Teaching games included: a bingo-type game highlighting Scripture passages associated with the events of Lent and Holy Week; a board game that lit up when the correct answer was given to questions about the symbols for Holy Week; a picture game in which the pictures had to be put in chronological order to show the order of events during Holy Week. The picture game utilized the line drawings from *Good News for Modern Man* which had been projected onto a wall with an opaque projector and redrawn by the senior highs—a real labor of love.

Poster boards were hung from the ceiling. Each poster board represented an important day during Lent from Ash Wednesday to Easter Sunday. Details about a particular day were spelled out on the poster boards so that the younger children who had not participated in the ongoing study could get answers to their questions.

Films on the subject from the American Bible Society were shown, and John and Mary Harrell's filmstrip and recording of "Christ Is Risen"* were utilized. A food booth served foods of the Holy Land, which had been researched by the senior highs so that the foods served were those probably eaten in Jesus' day.

The senior highs served as facilitators during the fair, helping the younger children to play the games, running projectors, serving food, and keeping things running smoothly. They devised a scheme whereby every student participated in a maximum number of activities. Prizes were awarded for participation— balloons with biblical characters on them, bookmarks with Scripture passages relating to Lent.

The Palm Sunday Fair was a success from every point of view. The senior highs learned a great deal while preparing for the fair, and other children and adults learned by coming to the fair. In a year-end evaluation, the senior highs decided that the Palm Sunday Fair was "the greatest." They plan to do similar things in the future.   □

*"Christ Is Risen" is an Easter celebration kit, including the sound filmstrip with printed narration and music. Order from John and Mary Harrell, Box 9006, Berkeley, CA 94709. Price—$16.00.

Activities for Lent/Easter

● by Mary Case

There is a certain mystery about the message of Easter. Children can know and understand this and appreciate our admitting that we do not know all there is to know about it.

Often when we are not certain of the message to relate to our children, we act as though we had all the answers and they will have them someday, too—as soon as they are old enough. We forget that part of the wonder of Easter is that we never completely understand it. It is a time to teach our families a trust in God and his plan and a genuine love for Jesus Christ.

Seven-Branch Candelabra

If the families in your church have used Advent wreaths, they know that children could use this means to mark the time until Easter and to keep their anticipation and enthusiasm for the season in focus throughout Lent.

If you wish to make these as families, use a bar of Styrofoam three inches by twelve inches by one inch thick. Give each family seven candles, the tallest a purple one signifying Christ's passion or majesty, or a blue one to remind us of his message of hope. A candle will be lit each Sunday of Lent, with the tallest and central one saved for Easter morning.

The following Scripture verses may be read, or an adult may tell the story. Take time to talk about how this Scripture relates to our lives now.

First Sunday: Matthew 4:1-11
Second Sunday: Mark 11:20-33; Mark 13:28-37
Third Sunday: John 15:8-17; Matthew 28:16-20

Fourth Sunday: 1 Corinthians 13
Fifth Sunday: Mark 14:12-50; John 13
Palm Sunday: Mark 11:1-11
Easter: Luke 24; John 20:1-19; Psalm 98

Follow the Scripture reading with discussion and prayer. You may want to use sentence prayers with one member designated to conclude the prayers each time, or you may assign members of the family one or two Sundays for which they are responsible for the reading and the prayer. If your children are very small, you may use a short prayer or prayer response each Sunday, such as "We thank you, God, for Jesus."

Symbolism

To some Christians the ideas of Easter eggs and bunnies need to be excluded from this religious season, but the symbols are traditional—often religious in origin—and a real joy to children.

Hindu, Chinese, and Japanese artists have portrayed the rabbit in connection with the moon. In Egypt the rabbit's name is *un,* which signifies *open,* because the rabbit is born with his eyes open. The moon to them is called the "open-eyed watcher of the night." The rabbit, then, is shown with the opening of the new year at Easter, or the opening of the new spring season when so many new things grow.

Many experiences in history concerned the symbol of the egg. Paschal (Passover) eggs were broken each year to portray the opening of the new year. Edward I left a record in his expense account of 450 eggs, stained and chased with gold as Easter gifts. At one Easter the pope gave Henry VIII an egg encased in silver.

The egg has remained a very real symbol in our time for a spiritual reason. We are aware of the element of new life within the egg; therefore, it is symbolic of the new life promised us in the resurrection.

Easter Food Ideas

Hot cross buns are a traditional Easter food. They can be purchased from the bakery or baked at home. The tops are browned and then decorated with powdered sugar in the shape of a cross and a thin white icing following the same shape.

An enjoyable Easter food idea for children to help prepare would be bunny rabbit biscuits. Use your favorite biscuit recipe or the small refrigerated cans of biscuits from the grocery store. Let one biscuit be the body. From a second biscuit form a small ball for the head, a tiny ball for the tail, and ears. Arrange on a cookie sheet and bake.

Make sugar cookies or another favorite rolled cookie recipe and cut them in the shape of an egg. Make plenty of colored frosting, or buy the cans or tubes of decorative frosting and give the children the opportunity to decorate the egg cookies as they wish. Nests for candy eggs can be made on top of cakes or cookies with colored coconut.

A favorite Easter salad idea requiring a little more work is to blow the egg out of the shell, making the hole in the top or on one side of the shell large enough to run water in to wash the shell. (See next paragraphs.) Stand the shells in their carton, fill with Jell-O, and let set in the refrigerator. To unmold, dip the shells quickly in warm water, crack shells, and peel. The molds can be decorated with cream cheese or whipped cream and served on a nest of lettuce or coconut.

Easter Eggs

Eggs are probably the most common symbol of Easter and possibly the most versatile. To be colored, eggs must be hard-boiled first or blown. If this is to be a traditional project, that is, one egg added each year, the blown eggs will be a necessity. If you have not tried blowing eggs, you will want to do this ahead of time, rinsing out the shells and drying them before the time to decorate.

Using a skewer or large pin or needle, make a hole in both ends of the egg, using the point to chip away a few tiny pieces to make the hole large enough. Push the point up inside the egg until it comes out with some yolk on it; otherwise, the yolk will not blow out. Blow these into a bowl to use later.

Eggs can be made to stand on plastic one-inch curtain rings or a one-half-by-three-inch strip of paper overlapped and glued to form a ring.

You can make a durable egg tree on which to add new eggs each year. Place your branch in wet plaster of paris in the container you want to use. Do not use a clay flower pot because the heat of the drying plaster might break it.

Make available to your families many decorating possibilities and suggestions. Eggs can, of course, be dyed with traditional egg dye or painted with watercolors. Model car paint is good to use because of its shine, range of colors, and tendency to make the shell more durable. If you have many small children working, you may wish to use some plastic or Styrofoam eggs.

If you are making a tree, the eggs can be hung with thread, yarn, or string knotted so it will not go through the hole; or with a pipe cleaner stuck through the holes; or even with yarn or rick-rack glued to the outside of the shells.

Tiny flowers, gummed stars and stickers, or small pictures cut out of gift wrap are good decorations to stick to the eggs. Your young people may want to try op art eggs. If you prefer to stick with religious themes, they can paint or cut tissue paper to paste on, making the egg look like a stained glass window.

Egg half-shells can be hung by rick-rack or yarn glued around the bottom and left as a handle over the top. Paint them as nests with tiny chicks or candy inside. Half-shells can also be painted spring colors and placed on the ends of green pipe cleaners to make a bouquet of tulips.

A good idea is to have your families review some of the symbols that might be used on the eggs to make them more meaningful. These can be painted on, pasted on, or done by Pisanki, as is still done in Poland today. This way the design is written on with wax by using a pointed stick or stylus, and then the egg is dipped in dye. The wax does not absorb the cool dye.

Some of the traditional colors and symbols are the cross (purple to represent majesty), blue (good health or hope), red (love), flowers (charity), white (purity of the soul), reindeer (a healthy life), hen and chicks (fulfillment of your wishes), the sun (good fortune), black—use paint or India ink—(remembrance), Chi-Rho, and dove.

You may never become a Peter Fabergé, the Russian goldsmith whose eggs of porcelain and jewels have become museum treasures. You may not be like one Cleveland, Ohio, family, which each year decorates its lawn with 9,500 eggs. But you *will* start a family tradition that will make Easter a more meaningful experience for everyone. ☐

Recovering Our Roots for Maundy Thursday

• **by Bradford H. Lyle**

Our church is a small congregation of one hundred people in Boulder, Colorado. For the last three years during Holy Week, we have held more or less traditional services of worship on Maundy Thursday evening in remembrance of our Lord's Last Supper. Though the attendance at these services had been fairly good, we had the feeling that we were missing something. This last year, we discovered what it was: spontaneity!—in a framework of preparation— spontaneity to let the Spirit blow where he would. We dispensed with the printed bulletins and rehearsed parts for this important evening. This year, we rediscovered our Judeo-Christian roots—and had fun in the process—by having a Passover-Fellowship Meal, modeled after the supper which Jesus shared with his disciples in the upper room.

Our common meal around simple tables consisted of roast lamb shank, unleavened bread, bitter herbs (we used parsley), salt water, and pitchers of grape juice for the wine—all donated by various members of the church. During our supper together the pastor and some of the deacons read three or four selected passages from the Scriptures which dealt with the meaning of the Passover event and the significance of the various dishes, as well as the meaning, from his words in the New Testament, which the Last Supper had for our Lord.

Our church members were encouraged to bring a brief Scripture or reading which helped them understand the Last Supper and to share these readings during the meal as they felt led. Three tables were set up in a U shape, and candles were placed on them. Our people listened to the Scripture readings and explanations as they ate, freely asking questions and making comments. We felt we had reclaimed the informal, spontaneous atmosphere which surely pervaded the original Last Supper!

After everyone had finished eating, Paul's words from First Corinthians regarding the Lord's Supper were read, and the act of Communion was observed in a very simple, quiet, yet meaningful way. To conclude our Passover-Fellowship Meal, the pastor asked if we could sing a well-known hymn together. Someone requested "Blest Be the Tie That Binds"; so we joined hands and sang the words together.

Our congregation felt good about this event for several reasons. First, this event being an informal kind of event centered around an actual meal, the importance was shifted from the number of people attending (which always seems the standard for any formal service of worship) to what actually took place with the group of people who did come. Rather than being concerned about empty seats as in years past, our attention was focused upon our meal together and its meaning for us! I have found this aspect to be important in a small congregation such as ours, where turnouts to special church observances such as Maundy Thursday are not numerically great, especially if they fall during a holiday recess.

Also, we took great joy and satisfaction in observing our members reacquainting themselves with the roots of our Judeo-Christian faith, symbolized in the lamb, the unleavened bread, and the bitter herbs which all point toward a God who in all ages delivers his people from enslavement and sadness! Our mood during this event was spontaneous and informal—our words and thoughts were in no way stiff or rehearsed. And together, sharing the same meal which Jesus had shared with his friends nearly two thousand years ago and following it with the act of Communion which he instituted, we felt his presence in our midst. □

The author was Pastor of the Mesa Memorial Baptist Church in Boulder, Colorado, when this article was written. He is now Pastor of the East Dover Baptist Church in Toms River, New Jersey.

EASTER

This year we wanted to emphasize the Easter event more than we had ever done in the past. Easter is our most important holiday; yet, it often goes all but unnoticed in our church school. In an effort to impress upon our students the significance of this sacred event, we decided to have an Easter Arts Festival in which the students could express creatively their understanding of the resurrection truths.

It is so easy for Christians to take Easter for granted. We forget to lift up the central ideas and present them to children in a meaningful way. We felt the children should have some factual input from the teachers and time for discussion and reflection before these truths could become evident to them; so we suspended the regular curriculum for March and April and concentrated on the Easter event. Each class study was to culminate in some form of artistic expression for display to the congregation on Easter. There are some suggestions about Easter in our teacher's guide for each age level, but we felt we needed more than that. So we prepared an Easter resource table in the church library. We put out everything we could find about Easter: adult books on the central ideas and books on symbols and celebrations in other countries. We found some filmstrips and records and some resources on worship and creative activities. We also have a well-stocked supply room with art supplies, and we had five "arty" resource persons standing by to help the teachers.

When we discussed the project, we developed six clues for creative teaching:

(1) Remind yourself that the chief goals of Christian education concern emotions, attitudes, and action patterns that reflect love for God and man, rather than the factual data committed to memory.

(2) Study the physical surroundings of your room. Try to make it exciting and different so that students sense the importance of the Easter study project.

(3) Use good art materials, and then forget about how good they are! Don't inhibit the students by saying, "We must not break a single big crayon. . . ." Encourage the children not to wear their best clothing, and keep smocks handy.

(4) If your subject matter or planned experience has touched the student with a real sense of relevance, your role in the art activity will then be one of giving direction and encouragement. Have confidence that, given the stimuli and the opportunity, the students will respond creatively.

(5) Remember that an experimental attitude is part of the creative process. If one thing doesn't work for you, try two, or three, or four.

(6) Remember that the finished product is not nearly as important as the creative process itself—the learning, growing experience which enables the student to express his or her thoughts in a creative way without restrictions of words or specified results.

When the completed work began to come in, we were amazed! The projects ranged from individual drawings and banners to children's spring gardens. There were elaborate class projects, such as the seniors' huge gesso sculpture, done entirely in symbols: a rooster (Peter's denial), a spear (Roman soldiers), a butterfly (resurrection), a pitcher of wine, a hand with a nail in it, a crown of thorns, and three crosses.

The senior high group also erected a seven-foot wooden cross on the church lawn. On Palm Sunday worshipers placed palms in the wirings on the front of the cross. After the Maundy Thursday Communion service, the cross was draped in black cloth. On Easter the worshipers brought flowers from home to decorate the cross. Luckily, we had a sunny day for the exhibit.

All the teachers, students, and the congregation were enthusiastic. We hope that this experiment has cleared the way for more experimental short-term experiences in Christian education. ☐

EVENT

by Jacquelyn Hall

The Promise of Calvary

by Dorcas Diaz Shaner

"The Promise of Calvary" is a series of dramatic monologues with one theme: the intimate reactions of those closest to Jesus immediately before, during, and after the crucifixion and the reaction of one witness to the crucifixion. It begins at the garden of Gethsemane and ends at the home where Peter and John are spending the sabbath. The monologues are intended to be performed as one play, but each monologue can stand alone and may be performed independently of the others. This series has been prepared for use by the local church and may be performed as elaborately or as simply as desired. It may be presented in the chancel as well as on the stage.

COSTUMES: The typical biblical garb may be used, or, for a different effect, you might wish the actors to wear contemporary dress. Your interpretation will be reflected in the clothing you select.

STAGING: No scenery is necessary. Simple staging and use of lights should suffice to set the mood. It is best that you place all of your characters on the stage at once, standing in frozen positions when they are not speaking. Each character comes alive, as it were, when his or her turn arrives, and one makes as full use of the stage as the director desires. Each character is assigned a portion of the stage and faces in a different direction from the others. Each player should take a stance and attitude in keeping with his or her character.

LIGHTING: Let your imagination be your guide! This play has been performed at different times with the aid of (1) candlelight, (2) floor lamps, (3) simple spotlights, or (4) elaborate stage lights. The most important thing to remember is the *mood* you are trying to generate.

A NOTE ABOUT MONOLOGUES: In performing a monologue, the actor will want to keep in mind that while no one else actually speaks to him or her, he or she must give the audience the impression that the stage is filled with other characters. Thus, head and body movements should correspond with the dots (. . .), which indicate a pause, often followed by a line which is a *response* to another character in the scene.

James

(A young man is sitting on the ground. He pulls his robes closer around himself. He yawns loudly and expansively. He seems about to fall asleep, but shakes himself alert.)

No, no! I mustn't fall asleep. The last thing he asked us to do was to stay awake. But I'm so tired. It's been a long day—or rather—it's been a very long week, and this garden air may be refreshing, but it's also lulling me to sleep. . . . Yes, I agree, John. I was as startled as you when he told us of his plans to enter Jerusalem on a

Mrs. Shaner is a pastor's wife and a free-lance writer living in Philadelphia, Pennsylvania. She is the author of a collection of monologues, stingers, dramatic duets, and one-act plays.

donkey. It didn't seem very kingly to me either, but the people certainly responded—all those palms and branches—and the singing and shouting—it was thrilling! It never ceases to amaze me how wonderful he can be with the crowds. Remember how he quieted those people stoning that woman outside the city gates? . . . That's right, I had almost forgotten that time when he fed five thousand who had come to hear him speak. That could have turned into an ugly incident, but he knew just what to do to calm them and take care of their needs. Incredible, isn't it? *(Yawns again.)* Peter, why do you think the Master asked us to wait here like this? Do you suppose we'll get to see him as we did that time on the mountain with Moses and Elijah? . . . That had to be the most wonderful experience of my life. I would gladly have stayed there forever. . . . *(Trying to make himself more comfortable.)* Oh, the trunk of this tree is really digging into my back. *(Moving.)* There, that's better. . . . *(Stifling a yawn.)* John, you seem so much closer to Jesus than even Peter or I. Why do you think Jesus was so sad at the Passover dinner tonight? And all that business about betrayal. I don't mind admitting I was very confused. He seemed so, I don't know, *different* tonight. Do you know what I mean? It was almost as if he were expecting something to happen. . . . Yes, that's what I sensed—he was

depressed. . . . Peter, do you understand what I'm talking about? Didn't he seem strange to you? . . . I'm glad you noticed it, too. It was almost as if he were saying good-bye when he said, "A little while and you will see me no more." Where could he be going that we wouldn't be able to follow? *(Exhausted now.)* Doesn't he ever tire? There he is, up there praying, and I can hardly keep my eyes open. *(Looking for a comfortable spot.)* I think I'll just lie down for a minute. It won't hurt to shut my eyes for a little minute. *(Falls asleep.)*

Peter

(A large man stumbles into view. He is obviously a laborer. His hands cover his eyes. He is in agony.)

What have I done? What have I done? The cock has crowed three times, and I have denied him just as he said I would. *(Angrily.)* I deserve to have my tongue cut out! . . . What's that I hear? Could it be the Roman soldiers looking for *me?* That woman did recognize me. What should I do? Where can I hide? *(Kneels.)* Here, this rock will give me some shelter. . . . Oh, Lord, don't let them find me. I'm so scared. Please, Lord, spare me. . . . Thank God they have gone the other way. But what am I saying? I don't sound like one of the Master's closest friends. I sound like a coward. Afraid for myself. Oh, agony, I never dreamed it would be like this. I was so sure I could stand up to anything that came our way. And look at me now—a spineless shell of a man. . . . And what did the others do? Did anyone stand up for him? I was willing to fight at first, even used my sword, but he forbade me. Then why did I run? . . . Why can't I be the rock he named me? I was so proud to be among his special ones. If he could see me now, he would die of shame. . . . *(Stands.)* At least I must not cower. I will try not to act the fool. ´. . . *(Quietly.)* How could he have known I would deny him that way? Does he understand the fear that I feel? *(Laughs a little to himself.)* Isn't it ironic, that I, who have seen him perform countless miracles, should question how he could know what a dolt like I would do? He told me, and I didn't believe him. . . . I was so filled with foolish pride that I didn't even understand what he was trying to say to me. . . . When those people around the fire said they had seen me with Jesus, something inside me exploded. I wanted to admit that he was my friend, but I couldn't. Something stopped me. It was as if my fear had paralyzed my brain so that I couldn't think straight. *(Covering his face.)* My shame is so great! Acting like this right after telling him I would follow him. Oh, God, right after telling him I

would gladly lay down my life for him. *(Kneels again.)* Forgive me, Lord, please forgive me. *(Bends over completely so that his face is hidden in his lap. Freeze.)*

The Witness

(This character may be portrayed by either a man or a woman [make the appropriate changes in reference to the husband and wife]. A native of Jerusalem, a peasant, moves to the center of the stage.)

(Raising right hand.) I promise to tell the truth, the whole truth, and nothing but the truth, so help me God. . . . I live in the city with my wife and three children. . . . Yes, I was there *(defensively)*, but so were hundreds of others. I really don't know why you had to pick on me. . . . That's a lie. I had never seen him before in my life. I just heard all the screaming and shouting and, like everybody else, was curious to see what was happening. Is there any crime in that? . . . Like I said, I heard all this noise, and I went to see what it was all about. Everybody was crowding the sidewalk; so I decided to try to look from my balcony, but that wasn't any good either because we live too far back from that

block; so I went back down again. . . . No, the kids had already left for my sister's house where we were all going to celebrate the holidays; so it was just my wife and I. She said she didn't want to be bothered with crowds; she hates crowds, says they make her sick. *(Gossipy.)* She never goes out in a big group if she doesn't have to. . . . *(Hurt.)* I'm sorry, I'll try to stick to the point. Anyway, I went back down and found my friend who always knows what's happening, and he told me all about it. It was still early; so I decided to see for myself. By that time the biggest part of the group had passed by; so we followed up the hill where things were getting started. . . . Are you calling me a name? Well, see that you don't: I don't go looking for gory scenes or get a thrill out of seeing blood and all that. Like I said, everybody else was going up; I just didn't want to miss anything. Besides, I had heard that there had been a big parade only the other day, and that the same guy was in it, and that it was *really* something to see. *(Pause.)* So I went to see. *(Turning.)* Frankly, your honor, I was very disappointed. I mean, the way some of them were talking you'd think the Messiah had come. All I saw was this man between two other men, hanging on a cross. So what's the big deal? When it started to rain, I went home. Honestly, your honor, I don't know why you had to call me to come here. There were a lot of other people there. What I saw, they saw. . . . What's all the fuss about anyway? *(Freeze.)*

Mary

(Mary is lying in a heap, as if she had remained where she had fallen after a long, exhausting walk. She looks tired and worn. She is about middle-aged, but suffering makes her seem older. She rises to her knees.)

(Crying.) My son, my firstborn son, why has God brought you to this place? *(No longer crying, but lost in reverie.)* Kings came to your humble birthplace to give you tribute. Angels sang of your coming. . . . *(Looking up.)* And look at you now—hanging helpless and worn. What has happened to my baby—the blessed One? *(Angrily.)* Are your accusers so depraved that they cannot see what is before them? Didn't they understand what you were teaching them? Some of those who listened to you preach on the hills of Galilee are the very ones who are taunting you now. And where are those who followed you, and loved you? *(Sadly.)* All gone—save John. Dear John. He is like another son to me. His sweetness is so comforting. . . . *(Cheered by a remembrance.)* My dear boy Jesus. You were such a rascal—getting away from me, and I thinking you were lost—always wanting to be with the elders, talking and asking questions. And *such* questions! The rabbis were really impressed with your knowledge. You coming from a carpenter's home— they couldn't believe such wisdom. But you and I know the truth. Not from a carpenter's home. No, my son, you are not even really my son. Born of my body, perhaps, but still not flesh of man's flesh or bone of man's bone. Who could understand? Who could I tell? Indeed—who would listen? I guess they would think me mad—or a fool. . . . All these years, watching you grow, I've known that you were mine for only a little while. But, son—why so cruel a death? My heart

breaks and wants to shatter the skies with its screams. . . . I waited all these years to see you crowned king. My darling, the *sign* reads "King of the Jews," but the Jews don't know you. Your poor crown holds blood rather than rubies *(stands as if to come closer to cross).* . . . Dear, dear son. What can I do to make it easier for you? If I could take your place and bear your pain, I would gladly give my body for you. . . . *(Trying to be reasonable.)* But you have your work. You always said you had your work. When will I see its fruits, dear one? When will I know with all my soul that those dreams were visions and those voices were from God? . . . What was that you said? "It is finished." *(Looking around.)* Oh, Lord, what is finished? Surely not your work—that has just begun. Your life? My precious—inside of me you will never die. You will live as long as this poor body can move. And somehow, I know you will live even beyond me and all the others who are here. So, dear son, try not to hurt too much. Until this is all over, Mother will stay by you. *(Takes a step forward and freezes.)*

Mary Magdalene

(A young woman moves to center stage. She has been running and is out of breath. She pantomimes knocking on a door. When no one answers, she bangs desperately.)

Let me in, let me in. . . . It's me, Mary. Hurry, please hurry. . . . Oh, thank you. *(Enters room.)* I ran all the way. . . . I'm all out of breath. I don't know how to tell you this. . . . No, I'm all right, at least I think I am.

(Breathlessly.) It's happened. Oh, I can't believe it, but it's happened just as he said it would. . . . No, I don't think anyone followed me; you are all quite safe. . . . I was very careful. But please, let me tell you. . . . What's the matter with you? . . . I am *not* hysterical; I'm just out of breath from running. . . . Thank you, but I'd rather stand. I must not stay long; there are others to tell. . . . Yes, I'll start from the beginning. . . . This morning I was taking the oils to the tomb—and when I got there—it was empty. I screamed, "Robbers! Robbers!" but of course no one heard me. I couldn't believe my eyes. Why should anyone want to steal my Master's body? I just fell down sobbing. Then—then I *saw* him. . . . He was so beautiful. . . . Yes, you understood me. That's where I was. . . . I am *not* losing my mind. He asked me why I was crying, and I told him that someone had stolen my Master's body. You see, I didn't recognize him right away. Then he said my name. Oh, Peter, you know how he can do that. . . . Why shouldn't I have recognized him then? Haven't I spent much time with him? Haven't I come to know his face as well as I know my own? . . . No, he didn't let me touch him even though I tried, but he said he had to ascend to his Father. Then he told me to come and tell you; so I just got up and ran, and here I am. . . . What do you mean the tension of the past few days has been too much for me? I know what I heard; I know what I saw. . . . Oh, Peter, John, it was so wonderful, I don't think I can stand it. But . . . where are you going? . . . Come back. . . . Don't you believe me? *(Crying out to heaven.)* Dear God, why don't they believe me? *(Freeze.)* □

Playable for Passion Week

SCENE: Chamber of a Roman official.

by Harry Farra

OFFICIAL: Well, Marcellus, are you ready to present your report about this fanatic, Jesus? You've been about it for a week now.

SPY: Yes, sir. This is probably the longest, most exhaustive report I've ever put together on one of the citizens of the State.

OFFICIAL: You think it's that thorough?

SPY: Without a doubt. I've gone over the evidence a hundred times. It all points to the same thing without a shadow of a doubt.

OFFICIAL: Give your report, then.

SPY: First, I talked with all those who were supposed to have been healed, and in every instance this Jesus had claimed divinity for himself as he did the healing. This is documented seven times.

OFFICIAL: Are they willing to swear to his statements? Are they that convinced?

SPY: Certainly. Each time he said, "I am the Son of God."

OFFICIAL: Go on.

SPY: Next, I interviewed about forty of the common folk about his teachings. There's no doubt that he's setting himself up equal to Moses and sometimes even above Moses. Several times he placed himself even above the angels. This isn't rumor. I've got all the testimonies written down.

OFFICIAL: Good, good. Any witnesses for us—ones that will testify to the sayings of Jesus?

SPY: There are at least ten who will offer exact testimony as to his teachings. It's awfully incriminating. It seems that his teachings are above the law of the land, to hear them talk.

The writer of the playable is Professor of Speech and Communication, Geneva College, Beaver Falls, Pennsylvania.

OFFICIAL: The net draws tighter. We'll have him on a cross within a week. Is there more? I'm pleased with your proof so far.

SPY: I spent three days sorting through what some of his enemies had to offer in the case. He's a genius at arguing points of the law. Where he picked up all that knowledge no one knows. And to think he's a carpenter's son! They set up all kinds of trick questions, but he wiggled out of all of them— sometimes leaving them with only the laughter of the people ringing in their ears.

OFFICIAL: How about his followers—were you able to break into the group?

SPY: It was tough, but one evening at a feast at a tax collector's, I infiltrated the group, pretending I was a relative of one of the servants. At one point I even sat with the Twelve and close enough that I could have reached out and touched that Jesus.

OFFICIAL: So you got some devastating evidence. You heard from his own lips.

SPY: From his own lips. I have here a ten-page summary.

OFFICIAL: Good, good. That's all we need. It's done. It's finished. He's through.

SPY: There's one more testimony.

OFFICIAL: Well, we really don't need it with all the others.

SPY: But this evidence is the most damaging of all.

OFFICIAL: Whose is it?

SPY: Mine.

OFFICIAL: Yours? I don't understand.

SPY: Yes, mine. For you see, I listened to convict and became convicted myself. Listening changed me. There is no doubt. This spy has seen the Son of God.

Forgiveness in Love

An Easter Play
• by Frank "Ted" Reid

SCENE 1

(The scene is a room in the palatial home of Chuza, the steward of Herod. It is Friday, at dusk.

MARY OF BETHANY enters slowly. It is evident that she has been crying, for tears still glisten on her cheeks, and she twists a damp handkerchief in her hands. She moves across the stage slowly, lost in her own thoughts, but turns half-eagerly, half-fearfully, as she hears MARTHA enter.

MARTHA is a small, brisk woman who moves decisively.)

MARY OF BETHANY *(pitifully):* Is it over yet?

MARTHA: It's over. *(She moves to the couch in the center of the room and begins to arrange the cushions on it.)* It was quicker than usual. The centurion said he died of a broken heart.

MARY OF BETHANY: So quickly over? Yet it seems I have been here for hours. I wanted to stay; you know that, Martha. I wanted to stay, but I couldn't stand to see him suffer so. Oh, Martha, what shall we do now?

MARTHA: We will go on as he meant us to. Help me with this sheet. *(She draws a sheet from a chest near the back of the room.)*

MARY OF BETHANY *(shocked):* How can you be so cold? He's dead, and you go on your busy way as if nothing happened!

MARTHA *(flaring, and it can be seen that she, also, is close to tears):* I have to keep busy! Besides, in serving her, I go on serving him. The couch is for his mother. I have to go on, one step at a time. I have to keep busy; I must not stop to think, or I shall go crazy. *(Begins to sob.)*

MARY OF BETHANY *(moving slowly toward her):* I'm sorry; I didn't understand. You're right. We must go on.

MARTHA *(brushing the tears from her eyes with the back of her hand):* Come, we'll prepare the couch together. *(Talking rapidly to keep from breaking down again.)* I wanted to take her to Bethany, but she could not possibly have made the journey. Mary, I have never seen her look so old, as if the life had gone out of her when his life fled, as though someone had pierced her heart with a sword. *(Alert to a sound outside the room.)* Hurry, here they come now.

(As MARY OF BETHANY and MARTHA finish adjusting the cushions and sheet, MARY, THE

The author is Pastor of the West Union Baptist Church, West Union, West Virginia.

MOTHER OF JESUS, appears in the door, supported by JOANNA, the wife of Chuza, and MARY, THE MOTHER OF JAMES. SALOME follows, carrying a few articles in her hands. MARY OF BETHANY stands at the head of the couch as MARTHA hurries forward to assist the other women in lifting MARY, MOTHER OF JESUS, to the couch. MARY OF BETHANY adjusts the cushions so that she is partially sitting upright. MARTHA goes to the door, and MARY OF BETHANY follows her.)

MARY OF BETHANY *(at the door, whispering to MARTHA):* She does look terrible. That haunted look in her eyes.

MARTHA *(whispering fiercely):* And why shouldn't she! She just saw her own son die. *(More gently.)* Come, help me fix something to eat. *(MARY OF BETHANY and MARTHA exit.)*

MARY, MOTHER OF JESUS *(tossing feverishly upon the couch):* Joanna, Joanna, that dreadful cry. It keeps ringing in my ears: "My God, my God, why have you forsaken me?"

JOANNA: Hush, hush, you must try to forget now.

MARY, MOTHER OF JESUS: But I cannot forget. I must remember. I must remember the way he looked in the synagogue of Nazareth, the way he looked upon the hillside in Galilee. That was my son, not that blood-stained thing upon that dreadful tree. My son, my son.

SALOME: You must try to rest now.

MARY, MOTHER OF JESUS: Where is John? Where is John, my son?

MARY, MOTHER OF JAMES *(fearfully):* She's driven mad with grief.

JOANNA: Don't you remember that he said that John was her son now? Don't ever say anything like that again.

MARY, MOTHER OF JAMES: Where is John?

SALOME: He went with Mary Magdalene to ask for his body for proper burial.

JOANNA: In my grief, I had forgotten such things must be done. I shall have to see what I have on hand to provide for the burial. Come with me, Salome; you stay with her, Mary.

MARY, MOTHER OF JESUS: No, no, I shall be all right. Go with them, Mary.

MARY, MOTHER OF JAMES: Are you sure?

MARY, MOTHER OF JESUS: I just want to be alone and quiet so that I can remember my poor son. Go now, and do what is needful.

JOANNA: If you are sure you will be all right.

MARY, MOTHER OF JESUS: My tears are all spent. My grief is quiet now.

JOANNA: Call if you need anything.

(As the women move toward the door, DEBORAH, the betrothed of Judas, appears in the doorway. SALOME, JOANNA, and MARY, MOTHER OF JAMES, speak almost simultaneously.)

SALOME: What are you doing here?

MARY, MOTHER OF JAMES: Haven't you done enough?

JOANNA: Get out of my house, you she-devil! You smell of treachery.

MARY, MOTHER OF JESUS: Wait, let her come to me.

JOANNA: But she is the betrothed of Judas, the betrayer of your son. She is not welcome in my house.

MARY, MOTHER OF JESUS: Have you forgotten that he prayed God to forgive them, even as he was dying? Let her come to me.

(The women stand rigidly as DEBORAH approaches MARY, MOTHER OF JESUS, timidly.)

I would be alone with Deborah.

SALOME: Are you sure it is safe?

MARY, MOTHER OF JESUS *(sudden command in her voice):* Go!

(The women reluctantly, with backward glances, leave the room. As MARY, MOTHER OF JESUS, puts her feet to the floor and sits upright, DEBORAH crosses quickly and falls to her knees before her.)

DEBORAH: I don't understand. I'm so confused. I didn't know where else to go but to come to you.

MARY, MOTHER OF JESUS *(brushing back the hair from DEBORAH'S face):* There, there, child. You are welcome here with me.

DEBORAH *(gesturing with her head):* But they hate me.

MARY, MOTHER OF JESUS: They are just as frightened and confused as you are.

DEBORAH: But they believe that Judas betrayed your son. I can't. For years, whenever I saw Judas, all he talked about was Jesus; what a change there was to be because of him! Twice he put off our

wedding day because he had to be free to follow Jesus. I almost hated Jesus because he stood in the way of my happiness, but all the wonderful things Judas told me about him made me love him.

MARY, MOTHER OF JESUS *(to herself):* He was loved by many, but not by all.

DEBORAH: And now they say Judas has betrayed him, betrayed the man for whom he sacrificed our wedding. *(Rising and pacing.)* I knew something was wrong. Judas had been telling me that something important was going to happen. He has been so full of excitement. And then, last night he burst into our house. He looked almost as if he were possessed. He stared at me, but he didn't see me, but some horrible vision. And then, with a terrible groan he shouted, "NO!" I tried to go to him even though my mother sought to hold me back; but he pushed both of us away and was gone. When I heard that Jesus had been arrested and condemned, I knew that that must have been what made him so wild. *(Turning sharply to MARY, MOTHER OF JESUS.)* But Judas betray Jesus? No, no one can ever make me believe that.

MARY, MOTHER OF JESUS: Deborah. *(She struggles to stand, and DEBORAH hurries to help her. Standing face to face, she puts her hands on DEBORAH'S shoulders.)* Deborah, I'm sorry,

but it is true. Those who were there last night saw Judas lead the arresting officers straight to Jesus.

DEBORAH *(turning her face away):* No.

MARY, MOTHER OF JESUS *(Laying her hand on DEBORAH'S cheek, she brings them face to face again):* Deborah, it is true. There would be no reason to lie.

(DEBORAH sinks down to the couch; MARY, MOTHER OF JESUS, sits beside her.)

DEBORAH: But—but—how—why—how could it be? I don't understand.

MARY, MOTHER OF JESUS *(looking at her hands in her lap):* Neither do I. There are so many things I have never understood; nonetheless, I had to accept them. From the very beginning, the mystery of it all. It was so—*(She breaks off, lost in memories.)*

DEBORAH *(waits for her to go on, then speaks encouragingly):* Yes? In the beginning?

MARY, MOTHER OF JESUS *(speaks softly; and as she continues, her voice becomes stronger, her head rises, and the look of grief changes to one of joy):* I was seated in my garden, spinning wool into thread, when I felt I was no longer alone. I looked up and there was a man. No, not a man, but an angel, for he had the look of one who had seen the face of God.

He said, "Hail, thou that art highly favored; the Lord is with thee; blessed art thou among women."

I was frightened that he should speak so to me, a peasant girl; but he spoke soothingly to me.

"Fear not, Mary, for thou hast found favor with God. And, behold, thou shalt conceive in thy womb, and bring forth a son, and thou shalt call his name Jesus. He shall be great, and shall be called the Son of the Highest. The Lord God shall give unto him the throne of his father David, and he shall reign over the house of Jacob for ever, and of his kingdom there shall be no end."

But I was mystified at this speech and asked him, "How shall this be, seeing I know not a man?"

And he answered me, saying, "The Holy Spirit shall come upon thee, and the power of the Highest shall overshadow thee; therefore, that holy one which shall be born of thee shall be called the Son of God."

Overwhelmed by what I had heard, I replied, "Behold the handmaid of the Lord; be it unto me according to thy word."

DEBORAH *(in awe):* And it happened?

MARY, MOTHER OF JESUS: Yes, just as he said it would. I carried him, my Jesus, in my body. *(Almost laughing.)* Oh, the talk in Nazareth. *(Eyes softening in love.)* But my Joseph, he believed me. He married me when he could have put me away. He stayed close to me all his life. With his own hands he took the child from my body and raised him as his own son. No father could have been more loving than Joseph. *(Breaking down again.)* Thank God Joseph never lived to see this day.

DEBORAH *(wonderingly):* This must have been what Judas saw in him. No wonder he could not put our marriage before Jesus! *(Standing up.)* No. Judas could never have betrayed him. I know it! *(On one knee before MARY, MOTHER OF JESUS.)* I'll find him. I'll find him and bring him here. He can explain all this to us. I know he didn't do it. I'll find him. *(Rising, she kisses MARY, MOTHER OF JESUS, on the forehead.)* He can explain.

MARY MAGDALENE *(appears in the doorway; wearily):* Well, we have done what could be done. I wasn't much help. Joseph of Arimathea went to Pilate. Joseph put Jesus in his own tomb. Not even all my tears could wash the blood from him. Now it is the sabbath, and there is nothing more we can do. *(Recognizing DEBORAH for the first time.)* What are you doing here?

DEBORAH: I'm not here for long. I'm going to find Judas so he can explain this horrible confusion.

MARY MAGDALENE *(coldly):* I can save you some time. I know exactly where he is.

DEBORAH *(eagerly):* Tell me. Tell me quickly. I must go to him.

MARY MAGDALENE *(vindictively):* Hanging from a tree near the Valley Kidron.

DEBORAH *(half-faintingly):* NO!

MARY, MOTHER OF JESUS: Mary, don't be cruel.

MARY MAGDALENE: It's true. He hanged himself and escaped us.

MARY, MOTHER OF JESUS: Escaped?

MARY MAGDALENE: Escaped our just vengeance.

MARY, MOTHER OF JESUS: "Vengeance is mine, saith the Lord." Be kind, Mary; she loved him.

MARY MAGDALENE *(wildly):* And what of us? Did not we love him who was the best, the kindest who ever lived, him whom her lover betrayed?

MARTHA *(entering):* What is all this shouting? This is a house of mourning.

(The other women can be seen behind MARTHA, crowding outside the door.)

DEBORAH *(sobbing):* Judas is dead; I must go to him.

MARTHA *(shocked, but still practical):* You cannot go. The sabbath horn has blown.

DEBORAH: I must go!

MARY OF BETHANY *(from the doorway):* But you will defile yourself. It is the day of the Lord, and it is against the law of God to touch the dead on the sabbath.

DEBORAH: God? I curse the very name of God! *(Women gasp. She turns to MARY, MOTHER OF JESUS.)* You said that your son was the Son of God, and Judas believed that. God would not let anything happen to his Son. But he is dead, and my Judas, too. What kind of a God is he that he would kill his own Son? I defy him! *(She rushes out, pushing through the women who follow her, trying to catch her and hold her back.)*

MARY, MOTHER OF JESUS *(alone):* He was the Son of God! He was! I gave birth to him, but he was never really mine. I never understood him. Oh, God, help me to understand how this could have happened. *(MARY, MOTHER OF JESUS, falls back on the cushions, weeping, as the women rush back to comfort her.)*

SCENE 2

(The scene is the garden near the tomb of Joseph of Arimathea. It is Sunday morning. This can be staged in front of the curtain or to one side to avoid shifting scenery. As the scene opens, MARY, MOTHER OF JAMES, and SALOME rush across the stage and out. MARY MAGDALENE follows slowly, as if dazed, to the center of the stage and stops.)

MARY MAGDALENE *(softly to herself):* "Why seek ye the living among the dead? He is not here, but is risen." But how can that be? Is it all some cruel joke? It must be. *(Weeping.)* They have stolen him away. Why couldn't they let him alone in death? Why must they deny me my last service to him? Perhaps they have hidden him somewhere nearby. I must find him. *(She returns from where she came.)*

DEBORAH *(entering):* You'll rest quietly here, my Judas, close to the master you served so well but so unwisely. How could you believe his mad idea that he was the Messiah, the Son of God? Look at my hands that you so loved to kiss. You told me one day that when you were a great man in the new kingdom, they would be covered with precious gems. Look at them now, covered with the dirt of your grave. None to help me. No one else cared. All day and night, pushing aside the stones that choked the earth, until my blood flowed hot and red as my grief. Now rest quietly, your heart no longer feeling from the mistake you made. All is quiet now, though the night was restless. How bright the sun, yet how dark the day! All days will be dark without you, the sun of my life. How grandly you used to plan for the kingdom to come, and now that kingdom lies in yonder grave. *(Looking back, she sees MARY MAGDALENE rushing across the stage. As she exits, DEBORAH calls out.)* Mary! Mary Magdalene!

MARY MAGDALENE *(rushing back in, out of breath, ecstatic):* Deborah, what are you doing here? Oh, Deborah, he is risen. I thought it was the gardener;

but he said, "Mary," and I knew it was he. He is risen! *(She dashes offstage again.)*

DEBORAH *(bewildered, calling after her):* Who? Who?

MARY MAGDALENE *(offstage):* Jesus is risen!

DEBORAH *(thunderstruck, she stands for a moment, unable to comprehend):* How can it be? Jesus risen? Could it be that he *was* the Son of God? Could it be you were so right and so wrong, Judas? Could it be that you betrayed the Son of God? No, no, it couldn't be. She's mad with pain and grief. I must find her. I must stop her. *(Exit after MARY MAGDALENE.)*

SCENE 3

(The same room in Chuza's house, a short time later. MARY, MOTHER OF JESUS, is still lying on the same couch. Her face is now peaceful and smiling.)

DEBORAH *(entering, out of breath):* Is she here?

MARY, MOTHER OF JESUS: Who?

DEBORAH: Mary Magdalene.

MARY, MOTHER OF JESUS: She has been here and has gone to tell the others of the joyous news.

DEBORAH: I must stop her before it is too late and she has spread this mad story over the entire city. *(She turns to go.)*

MARY, MOTHER OF JESUS: It *is* true! He has risen!

DEBORAH *(turning back):* She has convinced you of this insane thing?

MARY, MOTHER OF JESUS: She only confirmed what the others, Mary and Salome, told me and what I already knew in my heart at the break of day. He has risen!

DEBORAH: It can't be true. It's mad. The dead don't rise.

MARY, MOTHER OF JESUS: Believe me, it is true.

DEBORAH: But that would mean that Judas was completely wrong.

MARY, MOTHER OF JESUS: He was mistaken. He never understood, even as I never understood that my son was to be God's sacrificial gift of love to this sin-weary world, that his kingdom was a kingdom of the spirit and not of earthly power and splendor. How greatly we misunderstood him! When he seemed to be mildest and gentlest, teaching what was right in the sight of God, teaching that the meek shall inherit the earth, he was most powerful; and we could not see it.

DEBORAH *(running to her and kneeling):* How could we not have known? Where were we mistaken?

MARY, MOTHER OF JESUS: We were so wrapped up in our own ideas, our own hopes, your Judas with his plans for a mighty kingdom, that we were all deaf to his message. We could not begin to know the glory he had planned for us.

DEBORAH: But I cursed him; I blasphemed God; and Judas betrayed him. *(Sobbing.)* I am lost; he will never forgive me.

MARY, MOTHER OF JESUS: But he will, for he has not only brought the power of life over death into the world but also the gift of God's forgiveness free to all.

DEBORAH: Even to me?

MARY, MOTHER OF JESUS: Even to you!

(The other women enter.)

MARY, MOTHER OF JAMES: Deborah, have you heard?

MARY OF BETHANY: Of course she has heard; can't you tell by her face? Poor thing, you're so worn out that you're trembling. *(Comforting her.)*

MARTHA *(coming up to help):* Come, we'll fix you some hot broth. It will do you good. *(Taking DEBORAH'S hands to help her up.)* Look at your hands. We must get some ointment on them.

SALOME: I have some in my room. I'll get it. *(Exit.)*

JOANNA: Bring her to the blue chamber. It is the coolest in the house, and she can rest there.

(She exits with MARY, MOTHER OF JAMES. MARY OF BETHANY and MARTHA help DEBORAH to the door.)

DEBORAH *(over her shoulder to MARY, MOTHER OF JESUS):* I know what he has brought into the world: forgiveness manifested in love. *(They all exit, leaving MARY, MOTHER OF JESUS, alone.)*

MARY, MOTHER OF JESUS: Forgiveness in love. Loving forgiveness. That is it. If I had doubted before, I would believe now, for I have seen your power to bring life to hearts dead with grief and bitterness. Forgive me, my son, for all the times I did not understand, when I sought to hold you back because I was afraid. I was your mother, but you were not my son. You were the Son of your Father, God. If only I had understood then as I do now. My soul doth magnify the Lord. My son— my God is risen! □

I Was There!
(When They Crucified My Lord)

A Lenten Drama in Verse and Music

• by Doris Faulkner

> This drama was presented as a meaningful preparation for the Maundy Thursday Communion Service at the Catalina Baptist Church in Tucson, Arizona.

COSTUMES:

Biblical costumes could be used, although the drama might be more relevant to the times if modern dress were used. The centurion could wear an army officer's uniform.

SCENE:

The stage is bare except for a large wooden cross—rear center. The sanctuary lights are on as the congregation assembles, and the lights remain on until the organ prelude begins.

ORGAN PRELUDE:

A medley of hymns of the Passion, including "The Old Rugged Cross," "I Walked Today Where Jesus Walked," and ending with "When I Survey the Wondrous Cross," at the beginning of which the lights go down and the sanctuary is in darkness except for a spotlight illuminating the cross.

ENTER:

Simon of Cyrene, Mary Magdalene, John, and the centurion.

TABLEAU:

All face the cross, some kneeling, all expressing grief, except the centurion who remains standing, facing the congregation. Peter enters from opposite side and stands some distance away. He does not want to be recognized. (If biblical costumes are used, he might try to hide his face with his cloak.)

SOLO:

"Were You There?" (The soloists are not seen by the congregation.) All maintain positions during solo, at the end of which Simon of Cyrene advances to front center.

SIMON OF CYRENE:

I didn't mean to get involved; I'd business of my
    own.
But on the way to Calvary the Man had fallen down.
The heavy cross was far too much for his frail frame
    to bear,
And when the soldier ordered me, his load I had to
    share.
I helped him struggle to his feet. His strength was
    almost spent,

Mrs. Harvey Faulkner is a free-lance writer and an active member of the Catalina Baptist Church, Tucson, Arizona.

But when I tried to lift the cross, to my astonish-
    ment
The sins of all the world were added to its weight;
    and though
He uttered not a single word, somehow I seemed to
    know.
I picked his heavy burden up, and with him by my
    side
We plodded up that barren hill where on the cross
    he died.
But as he said, "Forgive them!" as he hung upon the
    tree,
His eyes looked deep into my own, and thus he
    spoke to me.
I didn't mean to get involved, for I had business
    hence;
But I have walked where Jesus walked, and oh, the
    difference!

(After speaking, Simon returns to his place beside the cross.)

MINISTER:

(John 19:25; Luke 8:2, KJV) Now there stood by the cross of Jesus . . . [a certain woman] which had been healed of evil spirits . . . , Mary called Magdalene, out of whom went seven devils.

(Mary Magdalene advances to center front. During the first eighteen lines of her speech she is recalling her conversion. She expresses grief.)

MARY MAGDALENE:

Magdala: city of sin and degradation;
He came there once, and saw me, dissolute,
Rapt in the revelry. (I lived for pleasure.)
Something about him captured my attention.
Was it his gentle strength? His dignity?
I only know I felt a sense of shame.
I looked within, and all at once I saw
The hollow burnt-out ruin of my life,
I'd been possessed
By all the ugly demons of the flesh;
But suddenly I wanted to be free.
Then, tenderly, he looked into my face.
           "Mary!" he said—that's all,
But mirrored in his eyes
I saw the woman I might hope to be.

Then one by one, the demons slinked away,
And for the first time in my sin-sick life
My fevered soul found peace. Yet here I stand
Beneath the cross where he in innocence
Suffers and dies for all the guilty world.
He knew no sin!
Now is it any wonder that I weep?
(Weeping, she returns to her place and kneels at the cross.)

MINISTER:

(John 13:37-38, KJV) Peter said unto him, Lord, why cannot I follow thee now? I will lay down my life for thy sake. Jesus answered him . . . verily, I say unto thee, the cock shall not crow, till thou hast denied me thrice.

(Peter remains some distance from the cross. He expresses his feeling of guilt and self-loathing.)

PETER:

Never can I condone my cowardice
   When I, who at the Passover had vowed
   To go with him to prison or to death,
A few hours later had denied him thrice!

He heard my craven lies in the next room.
   When the cock crew, he turned and looked at me
   In tender mute compassion for my shame,
And, weeping, I ran out into the gloom.

Even at supper he had tried to keep
   My blustering zeal from faltering, when he said,
   "I've prayed for thee that thy faith fail thee not.
And when thou art converted, tend my sheep!"
Then in the garden of Gethsemane
   When willing spirit could not overcome
   Weak flesh, three times I slumbered, though he said,
"Could ye not even watch one hour with me?"
(Turns and addresses the cross.)
   My Lord, I've failed thee! How can I fulfill
   What thou requested in that upper room?
   Help me, oh, Master! Give me strength to be
Thy willing shepherd, though unworthy, still!
(Falls to his knees.)

SOLO:

"Take My Mother Home!" (Paul Johnson) or some other appropriate selection.
(John advances to front center after solo is completed.)

JOHN:

With his mother I stood at the foot of the cross
   And he gazed at us tenderly
As he said to her, "Woman, behold thy son!"
   And "Behold thy mother!" to me.

She turned in her grief to my sheltering arms
   Where she laid her poor head on my breast.
Was it only last night, in the upper room
   In his bosom, *my* head lay at rest?

I covered her face with the edge of my cloak
   In order that I might hide
From her sorrowing eyes, the soldier's spear
   As it pierced his blessed side.

But even as Simeon, long ago,
   In the temple had prophesied,
Her soul was pierced by the self-same spear
   At the moment my Savior died.

She reached out her arms to receive her Son
   As they lifted him down from the tree,
And in anguish, she cradled him, as she had, once,
   In the stable, so joyfully.

The tomb in the garden was quickly prepared
   (For the sabbath had almost come),
And gently I said as they bore him away,
   "Come, Mother, I'll take you home."
(John returns to his place at the foot of the cross.)

MINISTER:

(Matthew 27:3-5, KJV) Then Judas, which had betrayed him, when he saw that he was condemned, repented himself, and brought again the thirty pieces of silver to the chief priests and elders, saying, I have sinned in that I have betrayed the innocent blood. . . . And he cast down the pieces of silver . . . and departed, and went and hanged himself.
(Mother of Judas enters. She looks around her, searching for the grave of Judas.)

*MOTHER OF JUDAS:

Alone, I search this barren Potter's Field
Seeking a new-made grave, where lies the one
Whose name throughout the endless years shall be a
Symbol of hate and greed and treachery.

It was not always thus; I saw him go
With radiant face and firm expectant step;
So honored, then, to think that he should be
Called by the Master; one of the chosen Twelve.

What changed him? When did Satan enter in?
Could he have followed any other way
Than what was written in the Prophecy,
Or was this, then, his destiny from the womb?

I saw that other mother weep, that day
At Calvary, and I wept, too, but ah—
My tears were even bitterer; for by
My son's betrayal, hers hung crucified!

It was a monstrous act he did commit;
Yet this was not to be his only sin,
For his remorse and horror were so great
He could not live to face his guilt, and so

He came alone to this forsaken spot
To add the crime of self-destruction to
His other deeds. And now he lies, unwept—
By all save me. This mother-heart of mine

Can never rest until at last I know:
When from the cross You raised your eyes and said,
"Forgive them, for they know not what they do!"
O Christ, did You not mean my Judas, too?
(Exit Mother of Judas.)
The centurion advances to center stage.

THE CENTURION:

This crucifixion's different from the rest;
　　That one between two thieves, what has he done?
All day, the mob has scourged and beaten him.
　　He's sure to die before the setting sun.

What sort of man is he? I heard him say,
　　"Forgive them, for they know not what they do!"
And I, a hardened soldier, pledged to Rome,
　　Feel something like compassion for this Jew!

Though they proclaimed him "king" in mockery
　　And placed a crown of thorns upon his brow,
He wears his crown in kingly dignity.
　　Even the mob is hushed and silent now.

He's dead. My soldier pierced his side for proof
　　Beyond all doubt. I'm glad it wasn't I
Whose task it was. Why do I feel this way?
　　So many times, *unmoved,* I've watched men die!

*Mother of Judas was published in two consecutive Easter issues (1959, 1960) of TIME OF SINGING, a Christian Authors' Guild magazine. Used by permission.

The earth is trembling! What is happening?
　　It's growing dark, and I am strangely awed—
This was no common man they crucified,
　　Truly, this Jesus was the Son of God!
(He returns to face the cross and falls to his knees.)

TABLEAU:

All face cross, some kneeling, some with arms outstretched.

MINISTER:

Were *you* there when they crucified my Lord?
Where did *you* stand?
Let us pray.

Dear Lord, We are gathered here, beneath the cross, just as were those first witnesses, so long ago.

Like Simon of Cyrene, some of us have felt the same indifference, the same reluctance to get involved. Speak to us; help us to walk in your footsteps and to feel the weight of your cross.

We all have been tormented by our own private demons. Help each one of us, like Mary Magdalene, to look into your eyes and see reflected there the person you intend us to be.

We would like to be like John, faithful to the end, willing to assume any responsibility you might require of us, but, like Peter, some of us have denied you. We remain far off, away from all the crowd, yet longing to stand up and be counted among your devoted followers.

Some of us, like Judas, have betrayed you in word or in deed. We earnestly seek your forgiveness even though we realize the enormity of our sin.

Strengthen our faith, we beseech you. We do believe; help thou our unbelief so that we may say with the centurion, "Truly this Jesus was the Son of God!"

As we gather around this table in celebration of that Last Supper in the upper room, help us to feel Thy presence closer than we have ever felt it before, and let the blessing of Thy Holy Spirit fall upon us.
　　For ever and ever,
　　　　Amen.

HYMN OF COMMITMENT:

"Beneath the Cross of Jesus"

COMMUNION

(Optional)

BENEDICTION　　　　　　　　　　　□

Death and Resurrection

The Easter event is at the center of our Christian faith.

Artists, throughout the centuries, from many lands and cultures, have expressed in a variety of forms their faith and their feelings about the death and resurrection of Jesus Christ. These artistic expressions provide us with a rich resource which can aid our own exploration of the meaning of the Easter event.

Included on the following pages is a selected sampling of pictures of creative expressions of Christ carrying the cross, Christ on the cross, the descent from the cross, the resurrection, the appearances of Christ, and the ascension. These can be used in a church school or youth group setting to provide a visual focus for the Easter event.

A variety of approaches can be taken in the use of these pictures.

- Have a six-week Lenten study on the artistic expressions of Easter.
- Have a special study on Easter or on some other day during the Lenten season.
- Supplement the lesson for each Sunday with pictures.
- Use these pictures to encourage the youth to draw

Christ on the Cross   *Georges Roualt*
20th century

their own expressions and even set up their own art gallery.

- You may want to supplement these pictures with others that you can find in books available in public libraries.
- Perhaps you would want to gather pictures of the entire Passion story and do an in-depth study of the entire week.   □

Resurrection   *Michelangelo Buonarroti*
16th century

Christ Bearing the Cross   *A. Dürer*
16th century
Metropolitan Museum of Art

Christ Carrying the Cross   *Omari*
20th century

Simon the Cyrenian, Compelled to Bear   *J. James Tissot*
the Cross with Jesus   The Brooklyn Museum ©
19th century

The Crucifixion
16th century

Albert Dürer

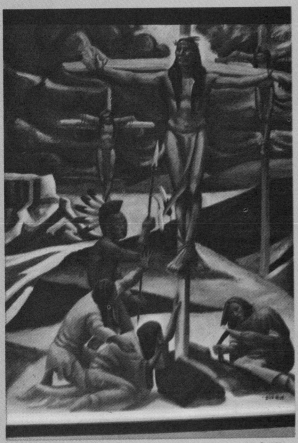

Fra Angelico

"Jesus Christ Appears to Magdalene"
Museum di S. Marco—Florence, Italy

The Crucifixion
20th century

Dick West

Christ on Calvary
19th century

This painting was shown at the Paris Exposition of 1889.

M. Munkacsy

Descent from the Cross
20th century

Painted by Luke Ch'en
Chinese Art

The Descent from the Cross
17th century

Rembrandt

The Ascension
  Courtesy of Three Lions

P. Mastroianni

Holy Bible

Interpreting Easter

A Symposium

In the following pages we have provided a
series of articles that will interpret the
meaning of Easter from various points of
view. This material can be used as sermon
material or in study groups

A Biblical Approach to Easter

Christ's Resurrection and Our Own

A Meditation on 1 Corinthians 15

• by David L. Bartlett

Paul writes chapter 15 of 1 Corinthians in order to remind the Corinthians of what they already believe. Along with the other early Christian churches they believe that Jesus was raised from the dead on that first Easter morning:

> I would remind you . . . in what terms I preached to you the gospel, which you received, in which you stand, by which you are saved . . . that Christ . . . was raised on the third day in accordance with the scriptures, and that he appeared to Cephas [Peter], then to the twelve. Then he appeared to more than five hundred. . . . Then he appeared to James, then to all the apostles (vv. 1-7).

The trouble with the Corinthians is not that they don't believe in Christ's resurrection. The trouble with the Corinthians is that they don't believe in their *own* resurrection. Their understanding is like the understanding which John Berryman expresses in one of his poems:

> I have no idea whether we live again.
> It doesn't seem likely
> from either the scientific or the
>   philosophical point of view . . .
> I believe as fixedly in the Resurrection
> appearances to Peter and to Paul
> as I believe I sit in this blue chair.
> Only that may have been a special case.[1]

Jesus' Resurrection—Not a Special Case

Paul insists, however, that Jesus' resurrection was not a special case. More specifically, Jesus' resurrection was a special case only because it was the first case. Paul writes: "But in fact Christ has been raised from

[1] John Berryman, "Eleven Addresses to the Lord—I" in *Love & Fame* (New York: Farrar, Straus & Giroux, Inc., 1970), pp. 85-86.

The author of this article is Pastor of the Hyde Park Union Church and Associate Professor of New Testament at the Divinity School, University of Chicago.

the dead, the first fruits of those who have fallen asleep" (v. 20). Paul claims that Jesus' resurrection doesn't simply show that God has conquered death for Jesus. Jesus' resurrection shows that God will conquer death for all of us: "For as in Adam all die, so also in Christ shall *all* [italics mine] be made alive" (v. 22).

When Paul argues with the Corinthians that Christ's resurrection is the sign that they will be raised as well, he is not just concerned with straightening out their theology. He is concerned with straightening out their lives.

Consequences of a Lack of Faith in Resurrection

Paul points to two important consequences of the Corinthians' lack of faith in their own resurrection.

A Frantic Search for Pleasure

For some of the Corinthians, that lack of faith leads to frivolity. They know that death is coming. They believe that death is the final reality for their lives. Therefore, they try to grab hold of as much pleasure as they possibly can. Their attitude is: "Let us eat and drink, for tomorrow we die" (v. 32).

That kind of frantic search for pleasure is not altogether foreign to our own lives. Sometimes we seek pleasure in chemical or emotional or spiritual "highs." Because we live in fear of death and life, we seek to set ourselves once removed from reality. Over against that search for escape, Paul says to the Corinthians: "Come to your right mind . . ." (v. 34). Paul insists that Christians, who believe in Christ's resurrection and their own, can face death and life in their right minds, without escape and without fear.

Sometimes we seek in a frivolous use of sex the pleasure which denies death. Sex is reduced to easy pleasure, a quick trick in bed divorced from commitment or concern. Since we fear that death is the final word for us all, we suspect that nothing lasts anyway, least of all any relationship. So we think that we can simply enjoy, enjoy; and if tomorrow we die, or weep, or ache with loneliness and abandonment, that's the way life goes.

Over against all such frivolous use of sex Paul insists on the centrality of our resurrection. He insists that some things do endure. He insists especially that loving relationships do endure. Paul believes that God does vindicate commitment and concern. Even death cannot overcome the awesome power of love (1 Corinthians 13:8-13). Therefore, Paul writes to the Corinthians who simply seek pleasure: "Come to your right mind, and sin no more . . ." (1 Corinthians 15:34).

Paul's belief that love endures shouldn't diminish sexuality; it should affirm sexuality. The faith in our resurrection and in love's enduring power should enable Christians to see sex as part of a rich and loving relationship, the marriage bed as a place of commitment rather than escape, and love as giving—not just getting.

Anxious Attempts to Prove One's Worth

Paul sees a second important consequence of the Corinthians' lack of faith in their own resurrection. Just as some Corinthians try to escape from their fear of death by their frivolity, so other Corinthians try to escape from their fear of death by their anxiety.

The frivolous Corinthians think that because death is coming, the future doesn't matter. People should grab all the pleasure they can in the present. The anxious Corinthians think that because death is coming, the future matters desperately. They think they need to forge their own immortality, to prove their own worth, before death does them in.

The Corinthians demonstrate their anxiety by anxiously trying to prove how wise they are or by anxiously trying to follow leaders who are wiser than they. They think that if they are wise enough or follow the right leaders, they can prove that their lives are worthwhile—even in the face of death.

We have other ways of trying anxiously to prove our worth, to gain our immortality even in the face of death.

Sometimes we anxiously try to prove our worth through our children. Sometimes our desperate attempt to prevent them from repeating our mistakes isn't really a concern for them; it's a concern that they should prove *our* value, guarantee our immortality. We know that we will not last forever, but in our children we will leave a splendid indication that we didn't mess up our lives. When they start acting a little messed up, then we get terribly angry at them because it is *our* significance that the little dears are threatening.

Over against that anxiety stands Paul's strong faith in our resurrection. Paul reminds us that our life, our worth, is guaranteed for all eternity by the sheer gift of God. We don't need to forge our children into the image of our dreams—because we are loved and vindicated apart from them. Furthermore, we had better *not* try to forge our children into the image of

our dreams—because they are loved and vindicated apart from us. In the light of the resurrection, we can stop being so anxious. We can do the best we know how, love the best we know how, and then actually *enjoy* our children. We can trust that God cares for us and for them as well, both now and for all eternity.

Sometimes we try to prove our worth through our work. We try to outfox death by the value of the jobs we do. We are terribly anxious lest we die without accomplishing anything of great significance. Therefore, we try desperately to achieve, or we rush anxiously from vocation to vocation, from project to project, hoping that we'll find the formula for significance. Most of us lose. Most of us end up knowing that the world will little note nor long remember what we have said and done here. A few of us win and look around us at the hurt lives, the painful ulcers, the moral compromises along the way. We wonder whether that significance was worth the cost.

Paul's strong faith in our resurrection also stands over against our anxiety about our work. Paul insists that the value of our lives for all eternity is not guaranteed by the work we do. The value of our lives for all eternity is not destroyed by what we fail to do. The value of our lives for all eternity is guaranteed by the sheer gift of God.

Resurrection Faith—An Invitation to Purposiveness

Paul's resurrection faith does not invite the Corinthians or us to laziness. Paul's faith invites us to purposiveness. It invites us to do what seems worth doing, not because our doing will gain us eternal significance, but because by God's mercy our doing can gain us joy and others good. Paul ends this section of his letter with the explicit reminder not to face death with pointless anxiety: "Therefore, my beloved. . . , be steadfast, immovable, always abounding in the work of the Lord, knowing that *in the Lord* [italics mine] your labor is not in vain" (v. 58).

It is just as hard for us as it was for the Corinthians to believe that God will vindicate our lives. It is hard to believe that death is not the final word.

Paul reminds the Corinthians—and us—that beyond death is resurrection. Paul reminds the Corinthians—and us—that Christ's resurrection is the promise of their—and our—resurrection, too.

That is why we can finally look death in the face without dismay. That is why we can live our lives without frivolity and without anxiety. We know that we don't need to vindicate our own lives. We know that we don't need to win our own immortality. In Jesus Christ, even despite death, God accepts and vindicates our lives. In God's love we have our final worth, both in this present life and for all time to come.

That is why the resurrection faith must always end in praise and poetry, and why Paul can say:

"Death is swallowed up in victory."
"O death, where is thy victory?
O death, where is thy sting?"
. . . thanks be to God, who gives *us* [italics mine] the victory through our Lord Jesus Christ (vv. 54-57).

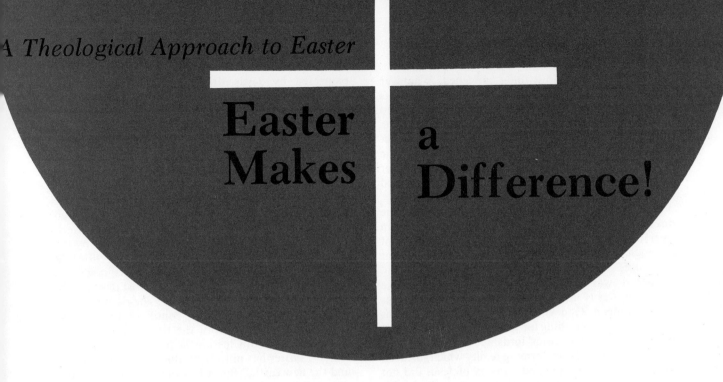

A Theological Approach to Easter

Easter Makes a Difference!

• by Alvin C. Porteous

In our modern, secularized culture, the triumphant biblical affirmations concerning Easter have been trivialized to the point where we are compelled to ask, "Does Easter really make any difference?" For many today, Easter is little more than an annual rite of spring. It provides some seasonal, ecclesiastical excitement which attracts a few more people than usual to church. But basically those who come are unmoved by it. And soon they are back to the humdrum of daily existence, little changed from having heard the glad announcement, "Christ is risen!"

For the early Christians what a different story it was! For them the resurrection was the animating and liberating center of their faith. It was a sign that the tides of history had been reversed and the oppressive powers of sin and evil and death had been overcome. It at once vindicated their faith in Jesus and mobilized their hopes for the future. For them Easter made all the difference in the world.

In our blasé modernity we seem to have developed an immunity to what someone has called "the threatening glory of the resurrection." The category of resurrection does not fit easily into our "business as usual," status quo ways of thinking. The very notion of resurrection is at odds with the comfortable, "surprise-free" existence of modern Christians. That is why it occasions both an intellectual and a practical embarrassment for so many.

Some theologians like Rudolf Bultmann have reacted to this embarrassment by reinterpreting the resurrection as a symbolic way of speaking about the deeper meaning of the cross. What we call the

The author of this article is Minister of the First Baptist Church in Lexington, Massachusetts.

resurrection was no more than the rise of the "Easter faith" in the hearts and minds of the disciples, these theologians say; the resurrection, unlike the cross, can in no sense be said to be historical.

Whatever else may be said of such a view, it clearly cannot qualify as an adequate representation of what the early Christians actually believed. Both the testimony of their experience and the "logic" of their faith point to the resurrection as a separate and consummating act of God's power following the crucifixion. It is clear that, for Paul at any rate, the resurrection is an indispensable linchpin of the structure of Christian belief. "If Christ has not been raised," he writes, "then our preaching is in vain and your faith is in vain. . . . If Christ has not been raised, your faith is futile and you are still in your sins" (1 Corinthians 15:14-17).

In at least three ways the Easter message of the resurrection of Jesus made all the difference in the world for the faith of the early Christians. And for the same reasons it is essential to the vitality and integrity of our faith today.

1. In the first place, Easter was a much needed *confirmation of the credibility of Jesus' lordship.* Following his humiliating death on the cross as a common criminal, his credibility, to say the least, was under a cloud. For the disciples the crucifixion was a crushing disillusionment. Their hopes "that he was the one to redeem Israel" (Luke 24:21) were cruelly dashed. Jesus' confident expectation that "the kingdom of God is at hand" (Mark 1:15) was exposed as naive and wishful thinking. With everything they had worked and hoped for now entombed with Jesus, there was nothing left for Peter and the others to do but to head for Galilee, back to the old fishing nets.

But then an incredible thing happened. Whatever the precise nature of the resurrection event (and there is room for considerable debate on this point), there is no mistaking the dramatic change it produced in the demoralized disciples. Later they were to talk about being "born anew to a living hope through the resurrection of Jesus Christ from the dead" (1 Peter 1:3). Something had happened which they interpreted as God's vindication of Jesus and his mission.

It is not simply a grammatical idiosyncrasy that the disciples used the passive rather than the active voice in their preaching of the resurrection. It is important theologically that they said, "He was raised" and not "He rose," in referring to the event, for what had happened was God's work—God's great decisive "Amen" to Jesus' message and mission. In raising Jesus from the dead, God vindicated his messianic claims and endorsed everything for which he had stood. Now it is possible to trust Jesus' lordship. There is now the assurance that the transforming reality which surfaced in history in the person and ministry of Jesus did not come to a discredited and ignominious end with his death on the cross.

Jesus has a future after all! That's the mind-boggling news of Easter that makes all the difference! Because Easter has clinched that for us, it makes sense to submit to him as our living Lord. Because he represents not "a dead fact stranded on the shores of time" but the wave of the future, we can afford to trust his authority over all of life.

2. Easter, then, authenticates Christ's lordship. But it does more. It provides *a justification of our hope for the future of the world.* The history of our recent past, in the wake of Vietnam and Watergate, has done much to generate a mood of cynicism and pessimism about our world. Many are prepared to believe that the future lies with the selfish and corrupt manipulators of power or with the impersonal and brutal forces of history which ride roughshod over human values and personal freedoms and make a mockery of love and justice. Easter makes the difference between that kind of cynical resignation and a hope-filled view of the future inspired by the resurrection.

It is a dilution of the Easter message to restrict it to its implications for the survival of the individual after death. For New Testament faith the resurrection is an event of cosmic importance. It is an act of the recreating power of God which opens up a new future for the world. In the death of Christ on the cross the powers of sin and darkness did their worst to nullify God's dream for human history. In the Godforsakenness of Jesus' abandonment on the cross it seemed as if the swaggering principalities and powers of the world had won the day. But God's "dark night of the soul" gave way to Easter morning. In the raising of his Son God's dream and his plan for his world were resurrected, too.

The cross and the resurrection represent history's most radical reversal. Whereas before the powers of death, oppression, and alienation seemed to control the future, now their future has been taken away. The future henceforth belongs to the "new humanity" pioneered by Jesus. It belongs to "shalom," the kingdom of peace and justice which he announced as being at hand. Those who struggle for liberation and reconciliation can take heart. Appearances notwithstanding, the future is open. It makes sense to hope. There is some point in working for social justice and engaging in political action directed toward a more human future. "For he must reign until he has put all his enemies under his feet" (1 Corinthians 15:25).

To be sure, the enemies of Christ are still very much on the loose. He is still being put through fresh crucifixions. History is still massively scarred by the horrors of man's inhumanity to man. Resurrection talk can be credible in our kind of world only if it stays in touch with the realism of the cross. Christ reigns, to be sure; but he reigns from the cross. The risen Christ is still the crucified One who continues to bear the stigmata of suffering until the final consummation. The resurrection of Christ is the first fruits of that final victory. Easter has not yet produced "the new heaven and the new earth." But it has authorized us to "hope against hope" that history is not destined to end in futility but fulfillment, as the kingdoms of the world become "the kingdom of our Lord and of his Christ" (Revelation 11:15). That mobilizing, emancipating hope can make all the difference!

3. "The last enemy to be destroyed is death" (1 Corinthians 15:26). Easter means, finally, *the announcement of our liberation from the tyranny of death.*

There are students of our culture who say that we are a people who are obsessed with the fear of death. And **that obsession leads to a massive cover-up of a reality** which is too painful for us to face—that we are all going to die one of these days and that everyone must die his or her own death.

Our Easter faith transforms the face of death so that it no longer needs be a terror to us. Because of the resurrection of Jesus, we can be assured that death, for all its threatening power, is no match for the power of God. Even more, the resurrection makes it clear that our individual personhood is not canceled out by death.

Beyond these rather modest affirmations, there is not too much we can be sure about as far as the mechanics of the resurrection are concerned—either Christ's or ours. Paul speculated about a "spiritual body" as the form of our continuing existence beyond death. This was his way of expressing the conviction of faith that our destiny beyond death will represent both identity and difference, both continuity and change, as compared to this life. We will be the same persons but also very different than we are now.

While this does not enlighten us much about the nature of life after death, the important thing to be able to affirm is that the individualizing love and care of God reaches us in death as in life. Paul's simple declaration in Romans 8 is enough: "I am sure that neither death, nor life, . . . will be able to separate us from the love of God in Christ Jesus our Lord." That assurance, born out of the heart of the Easter proclamation, is enough to make all the difference in the world in our struggle with "the last enemy"—death.

The Meaning of Easter for the Church as a Community

• by James E. Grant

Then Jesus told his disciples, "If any man would come after me, let him deny himself and take up his cross and follow me. For whoever would save his life will lose it, and whoever loses his life for my sake will find it" (Matthew 16:24-25).

I begin with the assumption that insofar as it is truly the church, any congregation is also community. We all know of churchy organizations which are hardly congregations, much less communities. In this article, therefore, the terms "church," "congregation," and "community" will be used interchangeably. The title of this article could easily be "The Meaning of Easter for the Christian Community."

If Easter is to have real meaning for any congregation of the people of God, it will be only if the day of resurrection is the climax of forty days of Lent. Too frequently, we free-church people have denigrated Easter by giving too little attention to Lent. The often used, even hackneyed, statement "There can be no Easter without Good Friday" really is true. If we would know the joy of resurrection, we must also know the anguish of death. The forty days of Lent provide an opportunity for Christians to give serious consideration to life-styles which deny Christian discipleship.

The traditional Lenten abstinence may be much too easy. Lent can be a time for serious reflection and self-examination in preparation for the Good Friday–Easter event. In other words, Lenten observance may

The author is Minister of the First Baptist Church, Elmira, New York.

be an important time to consider Jesus' words recorded in Matthew 16:24-25, printed above.

If Easter is to have meaning for the community of the people of God, that community must spend time in serious reflection and self-examination, using these words of Jesus as the basis for such reflection. But how may a church reflect on this passage? One possibility would be to try what Dr. James A. Sanders calls a "dynamic equivalent" translation. Thus:

Then Jesus told the disciples, "If any church would come after me, let it deny itself and take up its cross and follow me. For whichever congregation would save its life will lose it, and whichever congregation loses its life for my sake will find it."

How may a congregation know the meaning of Easter resurrection? Let it examine its survival instinct. How may a congregation know the meaning of life? Let it give serious consideration to the crosses it needs to take up.

Dr. Carlyle Marney talks about the self-denial mentioned in this passage in terms of having the "nerve to submit self-images." What images of the congregation need to be submitted to examination if that congregation is to know the meaning of Easter? Because communities of the people of God are historical, i.e., having a time and place, each congregation must give consideration to the unique self-images which need to be submitted for examination in the light of Jesus' cross. In general terms, some of the congregational images which churches must have the nerve to submit might be:

—*Success Motivation:* Have our congregations become so infiltrated with "bottom line" thinking that success has become an image (graven or otherwise) which we need to submit? Do we use the "numbers game" in enrollment, budget, or attendance as a criterion for discipleship? How does the image of success square with "taking up the cross"?

—*Earnings Ratio:* This image is similar to the success image in that congregations may begin to evaluate themselves on the basis of return for investment. Having invested a tithe—more or *less*—

does each member of the church expect some return according to his or her interests—good music, good sermons, good education, or some other dividend? Or does the community expect a profitable dividend from funds invested in the various denominational missions programs? Bluntly stated, can we support programs to feed hungry people without a subconscious expectation of a certain percentage of those people becoming Baptists? Can we give financial support to community concerns, realizing that the people served may never wish to join our church?

—*Name Brands:* This image has to do with the various labels we affix to persons. Those labels may be racist, sexist, "laborist," or "economist." How easily does the good, downtown, main line congregation with social status welcome persons whose labels are different? We Baptists congratulate ourselves because, unlike some other denominations, we ordain women and have women studying in our seminaries. How many of those ordained, educated women will be considered by the pulpit committee when next there is a vacancy? Does our image of ourselves in terms of the adjectives we use need to be submitted to the cross?

—*Real Estate:* How much is our self-image as a congregation tied to a particular piece of improved real estate? Have we made a graven image out of our building? Interestingly enough, many congregations are perfectly willing to cooperate with ecumenical endeavors as long as the meeting place is familiar. Union services are fine—as long as they are held in our sanctuary! Do all those brass plaques identifying memorial gifts "To the Glory of God" become images which we cannot deny to the greater glory of God?

—*Closed on Sunday:* A final image which we may need to submit to the cross is the image that we frequently have of the Sunday worship as no place to express emotions openly. Is it possible that the Sunday morning worship hour is the loneliest time of the week? Have we developed a pattern of polite repression of emotions—either joy or grief, anger or ecstasy—when the community meets? Has "peace at any price" become an image used to make board and committee meetings (or congregational business meetings) dehumanizingly unemotional?

We are talking about the meaning of Easter. My contention is that a Christian community will only appreciate the reality of Easter when it has submitted its self-images—denied itself—and taken up the cross. My intuition is that until a congregation submits its images of success, earnings, labels, property, and harmony to the cross of Good Friday, it will never know the meaning of Easter.

Easter is the time to celebrate resurrected life—the time of baptism or conversion—death to an old lifestyle and resurrection to a new one. If resurrected life is to have meaning to individuals, it will be only as they engage in the Lenten discipline of self-examination. If resurrected life is to have meaning for congregations, they must engage in the same Lenten discipline.

In other words, the old gospel song may direct the Christian community to the meaning of Easter: "If you don't bear the cross, then you can't wear a crown"!

Resurrection Experiences in Everyday Life

Edmund L. Kaminsky

An active member of Central Baptist Church, Wayne, Pennsylvania, where he serves on the Board of Christian Education.

We experience resurrection when we receive new life out of death. The death referred to here is not our creaturely death—when we physically and biologically expire—but death in a different sense, death in its ultimate sense. Ultimate death is separation from God, the creator, sustainer, and revitalizer of our being. We could use other words to express this condition of separation—sin or alienation, for example—but probably the best word is estrangement, which means that two realities that belong together have become strangers to each other. In the condition of estrangement from God we are physically alive but spiritually dead.

Spirit is what gives power and meaning to life. If we are spiritually dead, we have lost the meaning of our lives; and we have also lost the power to reestablish that meaning. The power to restore meaning can only come from God, who enters our spirit as the Divine Spirit. In 1 Corinthians 15:45 Paul says that the last Adam, Jesus as the Christ, became a life-giving spirit. This means that the Christ who is the life-giving Spirit and the Divine Spirit are the same reality. Whether we call this reality Christ or Divine Spirit, the presence of this reality in and to our spirit is the source of resurrection and new life. But our spirit does not exist isolated within ourselves; it is born in encounter with other human beings and receives and responds creatively to spiritual presence through the cultural and religious expressions of life.

Purposefulness

We look, then, for experiences of resurrection in everyday life. We experience resurrection when the emptiness, the aimlessness, the lack of focus, and the meaninglessness of our life become intolerable to us; and in the midst of that negativity we suddenly become aware of an ultimate seriousness and purposefulness rising out of our own depths to give direction to our life. Whoever experiences this has come into contact with the deepest reaches of one's own being, namely, the holy ground that undergirds not only all life but also, in particular, one's individual life. Our awareness of the ultimate meaning of life can be brought to consciousness through the actions of another person, a stranger or a familiar face; through an event, trivial or important; through something we have read, banal or profound. Becoming aware of the ultimate meaning of life does not produce a blueprint for action, but it does change the way we see our world, transforming what is old and stale into new and creative opportunities for growth into more abundant life.

Acceptance

We experience resurrection when, burdened by guilt, feeling rejected by life, and rejecting and hating what we are, we suddenly receive the certainty that God has accepted us. In this experience we know that the initiative has come from God and not from

ourselves. We are not told that our guilt is not as serious as we judged it to be, but worse; nevertheless, we know that God has accepted us in spite of it. We realize that God has not demanded that we first morally cleanse ourselves in order to merit acceptance; rather, he has accepted us in our uncleanness and declared us clean. Out of this experience springs a great love for the Divine, who has reunited us to himself; for others, whom we now see as the potential and actual recipients of the same acceptance; and for ourselves, whom we can now accept because a power greater than ourselves has accepted us.

We experience resurrection when, plagued by doubt, unable to accept the reality of the Divine, and resenting religious expression as superstition, we suddenly receive the assurance that we are justified in our doubt. In this experience we know that it is not required of us that we first start believing things in order to be given this assurance. Out of this assurance comes our openness to spiritual reality. We may not believe more than we did before this experience happened; but we know that an ultimate reality has taken hold of us, creating in us faith in its real presence and giving us the courage to live with and work through our doubts.

Encounter

We experience resurrection when we receive the power to break out of our self-isolation and self-concern into genuine encounter with other human beings. In these encounters we are forced to acknowledge the unconditional integrity of the other person, for we come to know that we cannot violate this integrity without losing our own in the process. We learn to look beyond all the differences that separate one person from another—age, sex, race, religion, personal dislike—and see a human face with its dignity, its problems, its need for healing. We understand that only through such encounters can we reach our own wholeness, for no one comes to wholeness in isolation.

Historical and Social Dimensions

We experience resurrection when we are empowered to overcome our absorption in individual and parochial concerns and move into the social and historical dimensions of our existence. In this experience we become aware of the essential unity of human life underlying the disruption in our world, and out of the power of that unity we receive the courage to battle the demonic structures that split and separate human beings. We discover our own responsibility to bring healing into situations of intense conflict, working always toward reconciliation and the restoration of harmony. In these experiences we ourselves are transformed, for we make actual our potential to create new centers for our lives, expanding our lives into new dimensions that can never be reached on a purely individual basis.

Unity of All Creation

We experience resurrection when we become aware not only of the unity of human life but of all creation as well; when we understand in their depth Paul's words (Romans 8:19-23) that the entire creation groans in travail and waits with eager longing for the revealing of the sons of God; when we understand that we ourselves, if we are led by the Spirit of God, are these sons of God (Romans 8:14); and when we actually experience the leading of the Spirit. Out of this experience comes our motivation to accept responsibility to preserve the environment; to protect its life; to acknowledge that nature itself, animate and inanimate, has as much claim for its existence as we have for ours. This experience informs us that we are stewards of the earth, not its masters, and that our own ultimate healing (salvation) and the healing of all creation are bound together.

Reunited with God

We know that we experience resurrection when we receive the power to pray, for we learn that prayer is not a conversation between two beings but the act in which the Spirit reunites us with God. We understand that words are not essential to prayer, that the Spirit can pray for us without words. Our spoken prayers only express what is conscious to us; but the Spirit roams freely through the depths of our unconscious, looks where we could not bear to look, brings our unconscious motivations to God, and elevates our deepest longings to the Divine.

We experience resurrection when, motivated by the power of the Spirit that has transformed us, we act as mediators of a new creation to others, bringing them to participate in this new state of things. Our witness is explicitly Christian, for we make clear that the Christ, present as the life-giving Spirit, is the source of this power. We make clear that our own new life is involved because Jesus as the Christ is actually what every human being should be: the human being in unity with God. But one human being could be in unity with God *actually* only if every human being is in unity with God *potentially*. Hence, Jesus expresses our own true being not as a remote ideal but as a historical reality. To be in union with Christ is to be reunited with our own true being. We express our true being when, like the Christ, we become like wine glasses, showing through our transparency the presence of the wine of the Spirit within so that those who look at us see, not us, but the Spirit within. Our life is new if it does not claim anything for itself but points beyond itself to the source of its power and proclaims in that pointing that estrangement from God has been conquered through an act of the Divine himself, expressing himself in human life through his Son, Jesus Christ.

We experience resurrection when, in the act of burying our beloved dead, we are struck by the power of Jesus' words to the grieving sister of Lazarus (John 11:25); and at the side of an open grave, in the depth of our grief, we receive the power to undertake our lives anew. In this experience we also know that we have surrendered our dead into hands more loving and more gentle than ours could ever be. We know that they are not alone in death, just as they were never alone in life. We know that their unique selves were affirmed, even before their conception, in the Divine anticipation of them and will continue to be affirmed in the Divine remembrance of them. Where our poor memories fail, the Divine remembrance endures forever.

We experience resurrection when, faced with the anxiety about our own creaturely dying, we receive the certainty that we shall never die (i.e., the meaning of our lives will never come to an end) because God has elevated the meaning of our lives to ultimate significance. Out of this experience comes our courage to accept our anxiety and to acknowledge with humility our creatureliness. We realize with astonishment that our individual life is a marvelous gift and that we are privileged to stand out of nothingness, to enjoy the beauty of God's world, to become joyous agents of the Divine work in human life.

These are examples of resurrection, experienced in our own here and now. Where resurrection is experienced, the deepest negativity is conquered, i.e., the power of death in its ultimate sense as estrangement from God the Eternal. Against this negativity stands the Divine Yes, creating out of this death a life which is eternal because the Eternal has entered into life in the person of Jesus of Nazareth, who is present to us in power as the life-giving Spirit.

Rachel Titus

A free-lance writer living in Mystic, Connecticut, and an officer of American Baptist Women.

I

Today I planted seeds of zinnias and marigolds. I have saved these seeds carefully all winter, for they came from the plants in our garden last summer. These seeds are the fourth generation of those I purchased in a garden store several seasons ago. I am sure they will produce flowers of the now familiar sizes and colors, and again I will pick the seeds to save them for yet another planting.

Today I listened to my small granddaughter playing a piece on the piano. Her mother taught her how to play it. But I had taught her mother how to make music on the piano when she was also very young. And Mrs. Mills had taught me with love, and warmth, and joy. In the music today one could hear the echo of her nurturing.

Every day we have these assurances: "Resurrection is real"; "Immortality is not a dream"; "God is present in all our life"; "Christ lives"! Every day we are in touch with resurrection; and when we are open—when the stone of blindness, or of pessimism, or of faithlessness, or of fear is rolled away—we feel the joy of its reality.

II

"Don't speak to me about the importance of goals," she said. "All I had thought I might be doing at this point in my life is now impossible." She was the victim of a stroke which occurred just as she was about to retire from a job in community service.

Serious illness has a way of making us change direction sometimes—or of stopping us where we are. A life that has been filled with service can suddenly become one that seems filled with the routine and the effort of merely existing. The future may be clouded and fearsome. Certainly the present is occupied with physical necessity which can become burdensome.

When such an illness is followed by recovery, one has the feeling of being given "a second chance"—a new life. It is a kind of rebirth, offering possibilities for taking new and perhaps more creative and productive directions.

Any serious crisis in a person's life can produce similar feelings. A person in public life becomes the victim of a whispering campaign among the townspeople. It eventually becomes so serious that as a result he/she loses his/her position. The person may be able to secure a position in another part of the country, but the person's health has been affected by the stress of the situation.

Retirement is often a time of crisis, not only because of the reduced income it brings or because of the prospect of empty days, but also because of the loss of self-identity that work relationships bring.

In our time people are living longer, and they often decide to make career changes in their middle years and later. Job changes and changes of residence are common everywhere in our country. The times of making such decisions are times of crisis. These and many more crises may confront us throughout our lives.

When a crisis is safely past, the decision made, the fear conquered, it is possible to move into the future with confidence. What a privilege this is when it happens! Everything has a new look! Values that seemed true and important will still add dimension to the new choices. New values may have developed that will affect the new choices. But choices there are, and a new life seems open to us. It reminds us of Paul's words to the Corinthians, "The old life has passed away; behold, the new has come."

III

She came from a country far away, a green and blossoming place, where she knew no need for dressing "in layers" to keep warm and had no knowledge of fireplaces and furnaces. In school she had read poems about the autumn in New England and the color and beauty of the falling leaves. She had read about the snow—how each flake had its individuality, how it could be molded into snowballs and snow figures, and how it covered the earth and made it white. She had pictured the coming of spring, with its new green life and its fresh flowers.

Yet, when she came to New England and began to see and experience these wonders that accompany the change of seasons, she realized that her understanding had been incomplete. Now, years later, she laughs as she recalls her discovery that ice is very slippery!

When the last leaves had fallen from the trees, although she knew spring would come, she could not seem to rid herself of the dread of what winter might mean, and she asked, "Are the trees dead?" The experience of the coming of spring that first year in the Northeast must have been a revelation.

No one who lives in a place where these seasonal transformations take place can see the coming of spring without awe. There is an almost visible movement, a fragrance; and the air itself seems full of color and sound. In Solomon's words, "The time of the singing of birds has come."

To all who see this rebirth, the resurrection becomes more understandable. God seems present in all of life. Hope for the future is possible. Spring is not only a season—it's more personal. It's a mood, a feeling, a knowledge of God's presence in every season. It can come at any time to the person who is willing to see and to hear.

"Are the trees dead?" When we hear of wars, many of them in the name of religion (Protestants and Catholics, Christians and Muslims engaging in terrible conflicts), we wonder, and are frightened. When hunger comes to so many of the world's peoples and threatens life everywhere, we wonder, and are frightened. And when personal catastrophes strike—serious illness, death of a loved one, loss of opportunities—we wonder, and are frightened.

Perhaps we can't appreciate a spring until we have lived through a winter. But the spring reminds us that resurrection, with new life and new hope, comes again and again and that we can be free of the fears that imprison us and interfere with our ability to walk where God leads us.

IV

"Who are you?"

"Oh, nobody much. I'm one of those no-talent people—can't do anything very well."

This was part of the conversation in a small group at a conference. The answer the woman gave is not at all an unusual one from a woman. There is a wistfulness in her answer; and yet she seems to have accepted the fact that she's "nobody much."

There have always been exceptional women, women of genius or of unusual energy or insight. There was Lydia, the businesswoman of Philippi who opened her heart to the gospel; and then her home became a center of influence and power in spreading the word in that part of the world. There was Harriet Tubman, a slave woman who led more than three hundred of her brothers and sisters to freedom. There were Marie Curie, Rachel Carson, Elizabeth Cady Stanton, Rosa Parks, and many more who made their outstanding contributions.

One of the exciting things that is happening today that has never happened before is that ordinary women everywhere, not just the extraordinary ones, are beginning to look at themselves, saying, "I'm somebody." A growing sense of personal worth is freeing them to use unsuspected abilities in ways they had never dreamed possible, for who women are and what they do depend in large part on how they view themselves.

This is not an easy thing for a person to practice. It means change in ways of living. It means accepting responsibilities that require effort and demand risk taking. Habits and attitudes may need transformation. It is no wonder that many women refuse to accept the opportunities that can be theirs.

A Christian woman who makes the declaration, "I'm somebody—I'm a child of God" feels in a new way her uniqueness as a creation of her Maker. She sees that every person is special in the sight of God. She also recognizes a personal obligation to fulfill her responsibilities as a disciple of Christ. This opens up new possibilities for serious discipleship. No longer is she "boxed in" by a role, limited by custom and old attitudes. She may find that this new commitment brings new tasks and a fresh view of her share in the work for which all people must be responsible. There is a new freedom to be and to do, to speak, to preside, to make decisions, to minister, and thereby to grow bit by bit to be the person God intended.

This, too, is resurrection. Here is truly "newness of life"—a rebirth of personality.

V

And so God reveals the meaning of the resurrection to us in fragments, over and over again. It is in all of life. It is in its beginning, with the birth of a baby—a new, unique creation. It is in its ending, with the new life beyond death that is to be.

The resurrection is in our hope for every day. It is in its despair as well, for the message of the resurrection is that out of death comes life. Everlastingly. Every day.

Henry Holcomb

City Editor of the CINCINNATI POST and a member of
Roselawn Community Baptist Church in that city.

Several years ago, I heard a Baptist minister begin his Easter sermon by confessing that he'd always dreaded preaching on Easter Sunday, that he'd always avoided the main message of Easter in his Easter sermons.

That fairly sophisticated, properly fed, big city, university area congregation began to get nervous.

I was a visitor, so I could have been wrong; but it seemed to me that many feared he was getting ready to mess up the wonderful Easter service—that he was going to announce he was surrendering to some secretly held doubt and quitting the ministry!

Easter sermons, he suggested, are too frequently a marketing person's dream, tailored to sell the Lord and the church program to all—or at least some—of those who haven't been inside the church since the previous Easter.

Thus, Easter sermons tend to rivet your attention on the cross, on how Jesus Christ died for YOU to forgive YOUR sins. And there's nothing wrong with that.

But the *real* message of Easter is the resurrection; and that's pretty hard to preach and listen to, the minister said, because one cannot accept the resurrection without experiencing a total and permanent change.

And change is—well, it's by far the most difficult experience I can imagine. I haven't succeeded yet; but that Easter sermon got me started, and I've been making a lot of progress lately. Maybe I'll even be living the resurrection before too much longer.

Trying to understand the resurrection has been difficult. To understand it, one has to understand death. And we're so insulated from death nowadays. People die in hospitals, surrounded by doctors and technicians rather than by loved ones or friends. Very few people I know have ever seen someone die. Funerals have moved from churches to funeral parlors, where the grieving family is protected from the view of friends and where it is said that the person "passed on" or "departed" or "entered into heavenly rest"; never is it said—that—the—person—died!

Accepting death means accepting a deadline for getting things done. Accepting a deadline means running the risk of feeling guilty when/if the deadline isn't met. To accept God's loving ability to forgive us for murdering his Son is to believe that we can give up feeling guilty. And oh, how difficult that is! To accept God's victory over death—the ultimate foe—is to give up our excuse for NOT TAKING RISKS in his name,—for—NOT—having—faith—in HIM, faith that he'll help us change ourselves—others—things, faith that he'll forgive us when we FAIL!

It means giving up our excuses for NOT:

• Being disciplined enough, orchestrated enough, and productive/effective enough to devote meaningful time to work, family, friends, church, the needs of others, the decisions we must help make as members of a free church and a free society, AND TO OUR-SELVES.

• Taking personal risks to put the most into and get the most out of life; for example, to develop intimate relationships with family and friends that enhance our creative and productive abilities.

• Being unselfish/courageous enough to examine our own lives and determine what our gods really are: what we would be most reluctant/unwilling to give up—whether it be some material thing, some role, some position of prestige/power, some minor freedom, even some pain/fear (I developed a strange affection for misery once).

• Listening to people creatively enough to understand their needs and fears and joys and even to help them understand. (If Christians fail to meet the Lord's deadline for bringing his kingdom to come on this earth as it is in heaven, I truly believe it will be mainly because we never learned to listen to each other and, therefore, got into many disputes and insensitive actions/positions as a result!)

• Managing our lives and institutions toward meaningful goals, all things considered, so that we individually and collectively GET SOMETHING DONE!

My journey toward understanding the resurrection has been, of course, deeply personal. Some episodes I can share. Perhaps you'll find them worth considering, even personally helpful.

———

When I was a youngster in my early teens, one of my idols was Congressman Brooks Hays of Little Rock, Arkansas, a friend of my father.

Shortly after the race riots in Little Rock, Mr. Hays, a layman who later served two terms as president of the Southern Baptist Convention, visited our home in Texas. My father arranged for me to "carry the congressman's briefcase" from Dallas to the state capital, Austin, then to sit quietly and listen while Mr. Hays and Governor Price Daniel, Sr. (also a Baptist layman) discussed how to prevent a Little Rock in Texas.

Mr. Hays was running unopposed for reelection, but

he was defeated by a segregationist write-in candidate. Surely he must have died a bit. But the courage and fervor with which Mr. Hays talked Christian political responsibility with Governor Daniel and the grace and humor with which Mr. Hays accepted defeat were for me early examples of resurrection experiences. His continued Christian witness, despite several subsequent defeats, have provided other experiences.

It was a hot, late summer Sunday in Texas, and I was really down. I had just returned from covering the 1972 Republican National Convention for Texas's largest morning newspaper; and my sinuses hadn't fully recovered from the tear gas outside the Miami Beach convention hall. My senses hadn't even begun to recover from being searched and corralled so many times each day by police and the Secret Service and from having just about every freedom restricted.

Before the convention, I had written extensively (with a colleague) about one major scandal in Texas state government; uncovered another scandal; and inadequately reported a statewide campaign in which all the statewide officials and half the state legislature had been turned out of office, partially as a result of the scandal my colleague and I exposed.

Even before that, I had covered higher education during the Vietnam War/campus riot years.

I was the model reporter; I reported everything that happened during or related to the campus riots and antiwar unrest. I developed the confidence of the students (antiwar, anti-establishment, anti-white, and, also, the silent majority) and of the campus police chief, campus chaplain, the faculty, the deans, and even the university president. That was no small feat. I managed the same professional coolness through the reporting of scandals and the political campaigns—I survived the conflicts, challenges to my ideals, the turmoil. Perhaps it was because of the notion my parents instilled in me—that every person has a role to play in the community. Mine, I learned later, was to be the reporter; the skilled observer and communicator; **the guy who got close enough to see, sense, smell, feel,** understand, almost live what was going on BUT WHO STAYED FAR ENOUGH BACK to report all sides to all sides.

But my strength faded after Miami Beach; and on that hot, late summer Sunday, I was dying.

My minister—the most consistently sensitive, open, unselfish, and prophetic pulpiteer I've ever heard—preached on freedom.

Only God's grace can set one free, because one is not free until he or she is liberated from fear, history, the inability to live with the imponderables, guilt, hatred, selfishness, weakness—and only God's grace can bring freedom from all of these.

That sermon was a significant resurrection moment. I felt free again to pursue my Christian responsibility of being a journalist.

After the award-winning first decade of my career in my home state, I left (for perhaps selfish reasons—a larger salary). To be sure, it seemed then and has since turned out to be a larger opportunity for service, a chance to become more creative as well as a leader.

But things went poorly at first. I strained for the extra base hits and home runs my ten years of building contacts and acquiring knowledge had permitted back home—and I struck out too often. My confidence faded quickly. A sense of guilt mounted rapidly. My frustration came home with me each night—all of my personal relationships suffered. More guilt!

Then one Sunday my minister, while teaching a church school class, reminded me that GOD'S GRACE IS SUFFICIENT! On what now seems like the following Sunday, he preached on Christian service through "creative followership" and "untitled leadership." Another resurrection moment—one that has had more impact over a much longer period and on a much larger group of people than I could have ever imagined then.

I said I've made a lot of progress lately. Mainly, I've specifically defined how I must grow to live the resurrection truly. I must grow—and significantly improve my ability to:

• Respond effectively to the special desires/needs of individuals in the following groups around me when I'm at work, at church, and elsewhere: (1) the most gifted/skilled/dedicated people; (2) the less gifted/skilled but hardworking/dedicated people; and, (3) all the others.

• Teach and share the skills/knowledge/insights I have gained with the diverse groups of people around me.

• Lead younger people to learn the lessons I've learned in a much more creative manner so that I won't have to lecture and preach so much and tell so many war stories. (Why can't I remember how much I hated being lectured to and listening to war stories?)

• Help those who follow my leadership at work and at church and elsewhere to make their jobs more exciting, to grow, to prepare themselves to accept greater responsibility (such as replacing me).

• Become a much more creative follower, to understand that my leaders are a resource that can help me get more done.

• Identify the good and bad things that happen in my individual and group relationships, then to build on the good and reduce the bad.

• Search for energy-/time-saving alternatives to the way we do things so that more can get done.

• Sense what's going on and what's changing around me, especially in the lives of individuals.

• Involve more people in leadership, planning, question asking, critiquing, praying, idea generating.

• Examine my own personal growth and progress in each of the roles I'm assigned to play.

• Think more openly: to deal more creatively and effectively with the moral, personal, spiritual, ethical, and professional issues that confront me or that SHOULD confront me.

• And survive, even enjoy life, on the cutting edge of change—FOR THAT'S WHERE THE RESURRECTION IS—without becoming pious, insensitive, cynical, selfish, puffed up, worn out—and without diminishing my ability to love and be loved!

Deepening Easter Faith with Audiovisuals

• by Joan Thatcher

Experiencing the Christian faith actually can be deepened through audiovisuals when the right tool is used effectively in an appropriate setting.

As many persons have discovered from good TV programs or theatrical films, professionally produced films and filmstrips focus the viewer's attention more sharply than most speakers do and often heighten the insights or emotions the viewer sees or feels.

One of the services offered by the American Baptist Films staff in Oakland and Valley Forge is to work with churches in recommending audiovisuals that would be most effective in a given situation. In this article we suggest three different plans that a local church could adapt for use during Lent and Holy Week.

In the opening scene of *Fiddler on the Roof* Tevye says, "Without our traditions, life would be as shaky as a fiddler on the roof." Lent is the traditional period of forty days and six Sundays preceding Easter. Between Jesus' baptism and the beginning of his ministry he spent forty days in prayer and meditation in the wilderness. Many churches recommend that each Christian plan a similar spiritual journey.

For the family Lent can be a time for conversations about the deeper meanings of the Christian faith, a time for discovering and creating symbols (such as nails and crosses), a time to reach out to forgotten persons in the community, or a time to make new friends at church. Selected audiovisuals can be the springboard to motivating family activities like these.

The author is Manager of Audiovisual Services, American Baptist Films, Oakland, California.

Another Face of Jesus

One interesting approach for a Lenten series would be to plan six midweek, Sunday church school, or Sunday evening sessions for adults or for families with older children. These could focus on various portraits that illustrate the face of Christ.

Appropriate filmstrips available from American Baptist Films include the Indian Christ, painted by famous American Indian artist Richard West, in *Another Face of Jesus;* * Asian artists who depict the life of Christ with great beauty in *Each with His Own Brush;* and fifty-three students at an American Baptist-related mission school in Zaire, Africa, who dramatize with great sincerity *The Passion and the Resurrection of Jesus Christ.*

A new filmstrip, *Frescoes of the Christ,* brings to life the teachings of a compassionate Christ. Six familiar scenes are portrayed by German villagers and painted by a nineteenth-century artist. You could use this filmstrip as one in a Lenten series or show the section for one painting each week, using the entire filmstrip at the concluding session.

Three motion pictures show other interpretations of the Christ figure. *Parable* focuses on a circus clown as a Christlike figure who is especially sensitive to the needs of others. *It's About This Carpenter* shows the reactions of New Yorkers as a carpenter tries to deliver a huge cross to a midtown church. *The Other Wise Man* is a moving portrayal of Henry Van Dyke's classic story of the fourth wise man, who uses his gifts for the King to help others in need and then, as an old man, returns to Jerusalem on the day Jesus is crucified. (This same story is also told in a filmstrip.)

"The Passion and the Resurrection of Jesus Christ"—The last days in Jesus' life, as dramatically enacted by students of the Evangelical Theological School in Kinshasa, Zaire.

"Nail"—If you found a nail like this in the street, would you try to make nail soup out of it?

"Another Face of Jesus"—A detail from the large mural in the chapel at Bacone College for Indians, "The Indian Christ in Gethsemane."

The Roads Jesus Walked

In traditional settings or in a contemporary style worship service, a teaching program can be planned that uses audiovisuals to tie together the various roads Jesus walked, with an emphasis on current Christian concerns.

"The road to temptation" could feature either a lively new filmstrip called *The Book of Jonah* or an air force commander's true story that is told in an outstanding evangelistic film, *The Conversion of Colonel Bottomly.*

"The Galilean road" can stress discipleship by using *Parable, Agape, Our Father, Our Daily Bread,* or *Somebody Loves You.*

"The road to Cana" could make use of *Agape* or the current motion picture *We Believe in Marriage,* which shows the dilemma of Christian parents when they are told their daughter is living with her fiancé; or the sound filmstrip *Frescoes of the Christ,* which includes a section on the wedding at Cana, could be used.

"The road to Samaria" or "the Jericho road" could be titles for discussing the importance of personhood and concern for the unloved. Audiovisuals recommended include two strong films: *Cipher in the Snow,* a film about a young boy whom everyone ignores; or *Peege,* a powerful portrayal of an aging grandmother visited by her family in a nursing home. Also recommended are the filmstrips *Shalom* and *A Matter of Stripes* or the film *I Don't Want to Get Involved.*

"The road to Jerusalem" could include a highly effective film called *Nail,* which tells how a young girl creates community in a rooming house; the filmstrip *Another Face of Jesus;* or *Courage of the Cross,* one of two filmstrips included in the set entitled *Jesus Is Lord.*

Appropriate for "the road to Calvary" would be the film *It's About This Carpenter* or the filmstrip *Cup of Sorrow* (see below).

Finally, "the Emmaus road" could make use of the films *The Gift* and/or *The Other Wise Man,* or the filmstrips *Alive!* and/or *Day of Gladness* (see below).

Audiovisuals for Holy Week

For more traditional formats the film staff recommends these films and filmstrips. *The Bible Story of Easter* is a set of two filmstrips in which professional actors recreate the Easter events in biblical settings: *Cup of Sorrow* relates the Last Supper, and the Easter story is told in *Day of Gladness.* This set of two filmstrips, with record, sells for $19.35.

Nail, Agape, and *Our Daily Bread* are three films that would be especially appropriate for a Communion setting on Maundy Thursday. For Good Friday the film *Espolio* is a sophisticated approach to the crucifixion, which is rich in symbolism and concerns the expertise of workmanship sought by the man who drives the nails into Christ's cross.

For an Easter Sunday breakfast you may want to consider *Alive!* or *Day of Gladness;* and for children, consider *Jesus Lives!*

Most congregations find that Easter is the high point of the church year and at its best can give a sense of bursting forth into new life. Effective use of audiovisuals can help your members deepen their faith in the risen Christ who told Mary Magdalene beside the open tomb, "Go to my brothers and tell them the news that you have seen the Lord."

---

* All the motion pictures and filmstrips listed in this article are fully described, along with sale and rental prices, in the 1978-79 audiovisual catalog, which is available free of charge from American Baptist Films, Valley Forge, PA 19481, and American Baptist Films, Box 23204, Oakland, CA 94623. When enclosing a check for purchase of a film or filmstrip, please add one dollar ($1) for shipping and handling. Reservations for motion pictures are made on a first-come-first-served basis. Especially for seasonal items, please order at least four weeks in advance, and give alternate dates or titles. Churches east of the Mississippi should order from Valley Forge; those west, from Oakland.